Seasons of
Reflection

Experiencing God
in the Great Outdoors

Tim E. Miller

IMD Press
Westminster, Colorado

Outdoor Reflections

Cover and interior design: Becky Hawley Design

ISBN 13: 978-0-9817335-2-4
Printed in the United States of America

Second printing 2009

Published by IMD Press
7140 Hooker Street
Westminster, CO 80030
www.imdpress.com

Contents

Acknowledgements

This book is dedicated to my wife, Lane Ann, and to my children—Grant, Jessie, Makenzie, and Reed. Thank you for allowing me the necessary time to experience God in the great outdoors. I have enjoyed every second of our time together afield. I pray you have learned to love God with "all of your soul."

To my dad, J.B.—thanks for introducing me to the great outdoors and to the God who created it all. Your contribution to my life will last throughout eternity. I will never forget the memories we have shared.

To Roger Tanner, my boyhood companion and lifelong friend—tadpoles, frogs, bees, rats, birds, and snakes, (and an occasional squirrel—don't tell your dad) all breathed a sigh of relief when we left town! You taught me a lot about sportsmanship and responsibility. My memory will always be filled with our boyhood stalks through "the woods."

To my brothers Daniel and Jonathan Carraway—the memories just go on and on and I can't help but laugh! Man, did we chase the critters or what? I love you guys. You shaped my entire sportsman's ethic and your dad would have been proud to call you "his sons." You have both grown into the men he prayed you would become. My life is honored to have been influenced by such a great man through you both.

To Billy Harris, Jerry Gaddy, and Roger Day—ya'll have treated me like a brother and I will never forget you. Time afield with you guys has made knowing Jesus all the sweeter. Thank you for investing in my life. You have taught me the true meaning of the word, "friend."

To Kenny Williams, my lifelong friend and turkey-hunting companion—your woodsmanship and ability to "bushwhack" ole tom has never ceased to amaze me. I was with you when you killed your first turkey and I hope I am with you this year when you bag your one hundredth bird. Thanks for all the hunts we have shared. They are etched in my mind forever—wonderful memories. You have proven yourself a faithful friend.

To Billy Hillman and Jerry Turner, my deceased buddies—can't wait to meet them again in heaven. They both contributed greatly to my life and not a season goes by that I do not miss them.

To my precious Savior, the Lord Jesus, who has made life worth living—I dedicate this small work to your Glory. You have blessed me beyond measure. I never grow tired of the beauty of your creation. Each new display reveals a little more of your glory I have yet to see.

Introduction

Every since my dad introduced me to squirrel hunting at the age of seven, I have loved the great outdoors. I was not reared in the country. However, I had one friend, Roger Tanner, who loved to hunt and we wore out several Daisy BB Guns chasing birds, rabbits, and other creatures. This all took place in a fifty-acre woodlot among the many housing developments rapidly overtaking the landscape. Roger and I both moved during our junior high school years. He moved to Louisiana and I moved to a small town in Mississippi. Things changed for both of us. Hunting land was readily available and needless to say, we both flourished in our new surroundings. Occasionally, we still call each other and reminisce about the "good ole days."

During those developmental years, I quickly discovered an intense fascination with all that was wild. Although I played a variety of sports, nothing came close to my passion for hunting and fishing. Pulling and backing a boat trailer were as natural to me as eating. Therefore, it wasn't unusual to see me headed to the river or dressed in camo driving toward the woods. I wore camo when camo wasn't cool. Before all the media circus began, I watched Fred Bear videos and listened to Ben Lee cassette tapes. Very few outdoor magazines could be found and instructional videos were scarcely available. I learned to hunt through the school of hard knocks and the patient mentoring of others.

Throughout the years, I discovered my love for God was greatly enhanced through outdoor experiences. I didn't completely understand what was happening until several years later. During a Bible study, I discovered God had given us the capacity as well as the command to love him in a multiplicity of ways. Jesus stated in Luke 10:27,

"You shall love the Lord your God with all your heart, and with all your soul, and with all your strength, and with all your mind."

Jesus is stating the most important thing in life is to love God with the totality (all) of your being. To love God with all of your heart means to love Him with all of your *emotions*. To love God with all of your soul means to love Him with all of your *consciousness*. To love God with all your strength means to love Him will all of your *motivation*. In other words, your motivation for living is to serve and love God. To love God with all your mind means to love God *intellectually*.

To love God with all of your soul (consciousness) means to love and adore God as you experience Him through your surroundings—or through creation. Many outdoorsmen experience a sunrise, sunset, rainbow, or sky filled with stars, and never acknowledge the author of its beauty.

Those who have learned to love God with all of their soul have learned to acknowledge and worship God through His creation. In essence, the outdoor experience becomes an act of worship. Although one enjoys the sport itself, he never loses awareness of the all-encompassing beauty and power of God's presence. He is glad to be alive to experience the wonders and beauty of God's creation and is not ashamed to praise God for it.

Some today would have us worship creation itself. This is not at all my intent. Creation points to the Creator. He has a name and we can know Him personally. His name is Jesus. I hope you will deeply ponder these devotional truths during your next time in the field. Should these thoughts lead you toward a deeper understanding of God, there is a section in the back of the book (page 157) titled, *How Can I Know God?* This section is designed to lead you into a relationship with God and get you pointed in the right direction.

I have learned many things about life and God while spending time in the field. This book is written for outdoorsmen (as well as ladies) by an outdoorsman and is my humble attempt to not only share my personal experiences but also teach others how to love God with all their soul.

Take the time to stop and reflect upon the things He has placed before your eyes. Spiritual lessons abound everywhere. Take this book out of your daypack and find an old stump or log for a chair or just stay in your tree stand. Unwrap your sandwich and spend time with God. Talk to Him while you are in the field.

Incidentally, every story described in this book is true and every character mentioned is a real friend. These devotionals were developed from over forty years of outdoor experiences. Enjoy the book, the great outdoors, and the God who created it all!

Seasons of Reflection

Can You See Him?

As dawn approached, the early morning silence was introduced by a canopy of stars shining over the Tennessee hardwood ridges. Soon a whippoorwill led off the morning chorus as other songbirds joined in. It was one of those perfect spring mornings every turkey hunter dreams about. Suddenly, a gooobbbbble joined the morning jubilee as adrenalin pumped through my body. I quickly moved to a spot closer to where the gobbler had awakened the sleepy morning while two other gobblers on adjacent ridges announced their presence.

Yes! This was what I lived for in the spring of every year. Finally, all three gobblers pitched down and began to majestically strut about seventy-five yards away. The gobblers were responding beautifully to my calling. One of them broke away and started coming toward me. Just about the time he was coming into range, he stepped behind a thicket and began drumming.

Moments crept into eternity…Pfttt-Dmmmm…Pfttt-Dmmmm… My mind was racing, "Where is he? I can't see him! This turkey is right here and I can't see him! He is so close!" Pftttt-Dmmmm…Pfttt-Dmmmmm…. I decided to softly purr and scratch in the leaves.

The gobbler continued to spit and drum for several more minutes—Pfttt-Dmmmm…Pftttt-Dmmmmm. One minute I thought he was to the right and the other it sounded like he was coming to my left. All I could do was wait—I was afraid to move. As hard as I strained, I simply could not see the turkey.

I could hear the faint yelping of hens in the distance. Eventually, he strutted and drummed out of hearing taking the other two toms with him. I suppose the hens coaxed him into their direction for a closer look at his majestic display.

Later that same morning, I killed a nice gobbler. As I quietly admired his spread tail fan and stroked his copper-tipped feathers, I became increasingly aware of the sights and sounds around me. Butterflies danced about, birds were singing as bees buzzed and buds bloomed. Suddenly, I became aware that all of creation was displaying a chorus of praise for the Master of all creation, Jesus Christ. I had almost missed it—I was too focused upon the details of the hunt.

If one pays attention every spring morning, he cannot miss the majesty of God. Indeed, I had invaded God's shrine of beauty in those Tennessee hills and almost missed Him! It wasn't that I didn't believe in God, I just didn't *see* Him. There He was right in front of me and I didn't see Him.

The next time the chill of the early morning causes goose bumps to rise up your neck and reminds you how good it feels to be alive, look around. Take it all in, and ask yourself, "Can I see Him?"

Challenge: Do you acknowledge God's presence each day? All creation testifies to His power. Do you merely believe God exists or do you have a personal relationship with Him? See *How Can I Know God?* (page 157) for more information.

Thought: What a tragedy to be so close to God and never see *Him*. Since you are afraid to move, He simply moves toward those who do respond to His majestic display of creation.

> *For since the creation of the world His invisible attributes, His eternal power and divine nature, have been clearly seen, being understood through what has been made, so that they are without excuse.*
>
> Romans 1:20

Life is Short

There I sat waiting—waiting for that unmistakable crunch of deer hooves upon the brittle leaves of the forest floor. Squirrels and chipmunks scurried about spastically looking for acorns, while leaves spun recklessly to the ground joining the chaos below. Wrens and finches added to the cacophony of sounds as the sun began to set.

I sat waiting and watching. But all I saw for hours was leaves—lots and lots of leaves—brown leaves and red leaves, yellow leaves and orange leaves—beautiful leaves. Suddenly, it hit me. Wow! What a brilliant display of God's glory!

How time flies. It seems like yesterday these same leaves were budding early in the spring. Some leaves hung tenaciously captive to their limbs as the evening breeze tried its best to set them free. Others let go rather quickly and spun to the ground. Some leaves drifted ever so slowly to their undeniable destination. Others made it half way to the forest floor only to get stuck in the fork of a tree. Where does it end—all of this spiraling, floating, blowing, drifting color? Eventually, *all* of them drift to the forest floor where they undergo decay. In so doing, they prepare the soil for the next generation.

Like people, leaves grow in stages. A small bud eventually grows into a leaf. But when buds are damaged by severe weather or browsing, they do not mature properly and die an early death—never finishing their intended life cycle.

Many people are like that. Due to some extreme experience during their developmental years, they never experience life the way it was intended to be lived. Consequently, they simply hang on as long as they can. Their lifestyle becomes a mere existence. Others never develop an appropriate purpose for their life and give up to the winds of difficulty. Their lives end in bitter disappointment and defeat.

Still others get stuck at the proverbial "fork in the road" and never make a definitive decision concerning their life's direction. Their lives are brand marked by wishful thinking. Consequently, some have long since given up on any quality of life and seem to be simply drifting toward death. What a waste.

From God's perspective, our latter years should mark the crowning purpose for one's life. Brilliance is the goal—just like the autumn leaves display. God desires us to shine like gold toward the end of life as we did in the beginning. Babies are naturally filled with laughter and joy unless someone suppresses such. Our radiance of purpose and spiritual well being should prepare the soil of life for the next generation. And we should do so with brilliance.

Faith in God makes it possible to do more than exist or drift in disappointment and defeat. The Grace of God empowers us to overcome the scars of our past and burst forth with renewed growth and purpose. Yes, life is short, but with God, it is never too late to begin anew. He is waiting to show forth His brilliance through you.

Challenge: Is your life drifting without purpose? Are you easily swayed by the winds of temptation? Are you leaving behind a legacy of spiritual brilliance and beauty for the next generation or mere religion? All of us will give an account for how we lived our lives.

Thought: I wonder if the angels can see the difference in believers as they slowly drift toward eternal life. I wonder when they observe individuals if they sometimes say, "Wow, look at that one! What a brilliant display of God's glory!"

> We will all stand before God's judgment seat. It is written, "As surely as I live, says the Lord, every knee will bow before me; every tongue will confess to God. So then, each of us will give an account to God."
> Romans 14:10-12

Don't Be Afraid to Laugh

I have always been passionate about turkey hunting. The sights, sounds, and smells of springtime are addictive. Throw in the thunderous echo of a wild turkey gobble and the results are intoxicating. A few years back proved to be an exceptionally good spring for me. I was hunting in a very heavily hunted public area and had already taken note of the obvious call-shy state of the gobblers. Around 10:00 a.m. I heard that wonderful sound of the tom turkey. Since I had already hunted in several states, the pre-season jitters were out of my system and I slowly moved toward my quarry.

This particular turkey did not respond to the regular run of calling. Therefore, I decided to scratch in the leaves and purr ever so softly. Eventually, I convinced him I was the hen he was looking for as he started double and triple gobbling.

I decided to shut up completely and pique his curiosity. Thirty silent minutes later, I saw him slowly slipping up the hill toward my position. He stepped from behind a tree at thirty yards and I squeezed the trigger. However, as the gun roared, I had the feeling of slightly pulling off my intended target. Much to my surprise, the gobbler starting flopping in that typical turkey dance of death.

I confidently walked over to my bird, placed my foot on his head, and unloaded my gun. I'm not sure *why* I unloaded the gun except it was a habit. I was congratulating myself on my hunting skills—"You sure fooled that ole tom, Tim. Yep, that bird is your eighty forth gobbler. Man, you are good. It's a shame no one was here to see that." I took my foot off the turkey's head to get a better look at him. As I lifted my foot from the gobbler's head, he was up and running like a bat out of the basement!

My first instinct was to shoot him again, but I had already emptied my gun. There was only one thing left to do—get him! The race was on! I chased my prize gobbler until I was close enough to dive on him. He inadvertently squeezed out to my left still on the run. I continued chasing him until I was able to pounce on him again, only to have him squeeze out to my right. I chased him until I was close enough to hit him in the neck with my gun barrel. The gobbler fell to the ground and this time I grabbed his neck and shouted into his ear, "I've got you now!"

Suddenly, it dawned upon me the absurdity of a grown man in the woods screaming at a turkey. As I looked at the endless trail of feathers behind me, I was overcome with laughter. I wasn't sure which was the funniest—the maddening chase or the echoing laughter that followed.

While regaining my composure, I tagged my bird, gathered my paraphernalia, and prepared to leave. While congratulating myself for due diligence, I picked up my shotgun and the barrel fell off! I stood there in utter disbelief with mouth a droop. This turkey had broken my prized shotgun.

Evidently, my adrenaline caused the gun to hit that ole gobbler's neck harder than I had realized. The retainer ring on the barrel that fits over the magazine had broken. Man, I was glad that wasn't caught on video! The entire hunt was a great lesson in humility.

I am very grateful for the gift of laughter. Christian hunters should be the happiest group of the lot because we understand the joy of knowing the Creator. Don't be afraid to laugh…especially at yourself!

Challenge: Laughter really does make the hunt fun. Has your seriousness about hunting excluded laughter from your quests? Is laughter a viable part of your family life? Do others see you as a jovial person? Talk to God about your answers.

Thought: Don't get so driven toward the kill that you forget to enjoy the hunt.

There is a time for everything and a season for every activity under heaven...a time to weep and a time to laugh.

Ecclesiastes 3:1, 4

Standing Out

One afternoon while scouting for an evening bow hunt, I noticed a beautiful soybean field surrounded by big timber—definitely an area I wanted to check out further. The September air was crisp and cool and I was delighted to be out on such a beautiful afternoon.

As I entered the edge of the field, I noticed something different standing in the middle of the beans. At such a distance, I could not tell if the object in question was a deer, another person, or some sort of plant. Upon closer inspection, I discovered a fully mature corn stalk. Apparently, the corn seed had germinated voluntarily or was somehow mixed into the bean seeds before planting. At any rate, there were no other stalks present—just this one stalk pridefully reaching into the sky.

The corn stalk had already tasseled and several mature ears of corn were visible. I suppose the nearby corn fields had aided in pollination. The soybeans were rooted in the same soil as the corn. Yet, the corn stood much taller than the rest. The soybeans had fruit in keeping with their kind but the corn stalk bore something totally different. The soybeans looked exactly alike, but the corn stalk stood out like stars in the midnight sky.

I asked God to allow my life to be like that cornstalk—straight, uncompromising, and full of fruit. How many times had I been lost in a sea of people never to stand up and be counted—never to stand up and let my voice be heard or convictions known? How many times had I laughed at the "off color" joke afraid of offending someone if I didn't take part?

For me, the cornstalk was a clear depiction of a life lived without compromise—an individual not afraid to stand out. I wanted to stand out among the rest displaying the fruit that only God could produce. I wanted to spring forth from the same soil of life as everyone else only to be different in resolve and purpose. I wanted others to notice something different about my life and I would never again be contented with merely blending in with the rest.

Challenge: What about you? Do you stand out? Do you blend in with the crowd or are you different? Are you firmly rooted in Jesus bearing fruit for Him or from the world? Are you living for *your* purposes or God's?

Thought: You cannot stand up *for* Christ unless you are rooted *in* Christ.

Thus, by their fruit you will recognize them.   *Matthew 7:20*

The Squirreliness of Squirrels

Have you ever noticed how squirrels are always in a hurry? Maybe it's just because they think something is about to swoop down and make an evening meal out of them. Maybe it's because the weather is about to change and they are scurrying about trying to take care of business before the front moves in. Have you ever seen the proverbial high limb act where the squirrel jumps with acrobatic skill only to land on a rotten limb? They can make quite a wallop on the forest floor can't they?

Squirrels are loud obnoxious little creatures and can be very entertaining. When I was a kid we called them "limb rats." Squirrels are the clowns of the forests—doing the craziest things simply because it is their nature to be "squirrelly." Many times at point blank range, they have stared directly into my head net daring me to move. You don't know if they really are going to jump on your head or they are just kidding.

They really are comical little creatures and can help hours pass quickly while sitting in a tree stand. Have you ever watched a squirrel run the same pattern over and over again—same log—same stump—same oak tree—same limb on same oak tree, etc. It's really interesting to watch them energetically dig a hole and then with gentle finesse pat the leaves down around the opening. I have been told squirrels never eat many of those nuts they bury, but manage to plant a lot of oak trees due to their spastic digging. As the sun sets, they scurry once again to their leafy nest or den tree where they curl up in the warmth and security of home. They are perfectly contented to live the life of a squirrel. They seem to simply love life.

I wonder sometimes how we must look running wildly about trying to meet deadlines and appointments. How many days do we run the same rut wondering if there is any benefit to it all? Maybe we feel like the competition is swooping away our business, or our boss is out to get us. Ever felt like you were digging a hole without purpose? Have you ever "climbed out on a limb" thinking it safe only to have it break beneath the weight of betrayal or compromise? Hurts when you hit bottom doesn't it? Squirrels seem to take it all in stride and hop right back up and off they go. Seems like they *know* part of hopping out on a limb is occasionally falling off. We are slower to recover from our falls.

After all of our barking, climbing, jumping, and digging—do we find purpose? After the sun sets, do we go home to a hot meal and climb into bed with a clear conscience? A state of satisfaction and contentment in life is extremely rare these days. Statistics tell us most men are not happy with their jobs. It seems this dissatisfaction creates an endless merry-go-round of existence. It's enough to drive you nuts. Is contentment really that far away? Learn a lesson from the squirrels—they live the life squirrels were created to live. What makes your life worth living? Are you living the life God ordained for you?

Challenge: In all your busyness, do you find purpose? What is your purpose? Are you contented with life? Are you truly living or merely existing? When you climb into bed each night, are you overcome with stress, problems, and broken relationships? Do you have trouble drifting off to sleep? Talk to God about your answers.

Thoughts: If you don't get anything else done today, choose to walk with God. He will transform the routine into an adventure! Through God's grace, even the holes you have dug for yourself can produce fruit.

I came that they might have life, and might have it abundantly.

John 10:10

The End Result

I enjoy shooting a bow and arrow. I have killed numerous animals with a compound as well as using traditional equipment. I am not a purest in the sense of having to use a particular kind of equipment. However, I must admit as I have gotten older, the *way* I harvest an animal is more important to me than *if* I harvest an animal. Consequently, I greatly enjoy the use of traditional equipment.

Last fall, I was preparing for a hunt by sharpening my broad heads. I envisioned that nice buck or doe walking directly beneath my stand. As I honed each edge to a razor's sharpness, I formed a mental picture of shooting completely through my quarry.

During the second week of archery season that dream came to test. I was sitting patiently in my hang-on stand when several bucks appeared on an adjacent ridge. Slowly, they ambled along picking up acorns. All of a sudden the biggest buck, a nice eight pointer, started angling toward me walking in a rather fast gate. If he continued, the trail would bring him directly beneath my tree for a perfect nine yard quartering away shot.

About half way down the trail, the buck stopped and sniffed the air. He stood there about thirty seconds before continuing down the path. "Please God, let him come down this path," I whispered. My heart was beating out of my chest as I anticipated the long awaited shot. The buck continued to close the distance—thirty yards—twenty yards—ten yards. Without thinking, I drew my 62 lb. longbow and released the wooden arrow shaft tipped with my razor sharp broad head. That distinctive thump when an arrow enters an animal followed my release. The arrow passed completely through the animal. The eight pointer jumped and ran about forty yards before coming to a stop. I watched in elation as the buck stumbled and fell to the ground.

I shot the deer through the liver and the left lung. He was down! Man, was that exciting! I had to sit down so I wouldn't fall out of the tree. How I love that feeling! I sat and replayed the event over and over in my mind before climbing down to field dress the buck. I hope I never get too old to experience those childlike feelings of excitement. When things come together like that hunt did, it makes all the practice and hard work worthwhile. It takes a lot of work to be successful, but the end result is worth it.

Challenge: Arrows must be straight and broad heads must be sharp. If you have children, how much time are you putting into sharpening them as arrows in your quiver? Have you prepared them to be released into the great unknown without a target or focus? Are you sharpening them to be an instrument in God's army? Have you tuned them to be shot straight and true from God's bow?

Thought: After the arrow is shot from your bow, it is too late to retrieve it. It will fly in the direction you have pointed it—so it is with children.

> *Like arrows in the hand of a warrior, so are the children of one's youth.*   *Psalm 127:4*

> *And the words, which I am commanding you today, shall be on your heart; and you shall teach* [this word "teach" means to sharpen through instruction—TM] *them diligently to your sons...*
>   *Deuteronomy 6:6-7*

Tough Shots

Practice, practice, practice—I practiced shooting my Ruger 300 Magnum all summer long in preparation for my first elk hunt. I had always dreamed of going out West to hunt the great Wapiti. However, being raised a "flatlander" from the South, I had never shot at an animal more than 150 yards. My rifle could hit accurately out to 450 yards, but mentally accepting this distance was an altogether different story. Four hundred yards—are you kidding me? An elk at 400 yards with the naked eye looks like a fly on the end of your barrel! I didn't think I could hit a target that far away. However, I eventually overcame my mental paralysis and developed confidence shooting at such distances. I was "ready" when the day arrived.

Here I was in beautiful northwestern Colorado on a crisp October morning. My guide and I had hardly made it to my stand when we saw elk climbing the ridge below us. A lone 6X6 bull quartered toward us climbing an adjacent ridge. I was trying to get situated and catch my breath as I prepared for the shot. As I quickly pulled out the telescopic legs of my bi-pod, the bull wasn't wasting any time climbing the mountain. He still had not detected us. As I struggled trying to find level ground for the bi-pod, it became apparent I would not be able to find such. Each time I located the bull in my scope, the cross hairs were crooked as I placed my bi-pod on the slopping angle of the mountainside. I ranged the bull at 412 yards. Suddenly, the bull stopped and looked directly at us. Since the angle was right, my guide instructed me to shoot as soon as possible. I carefully rocked my rifle onto one leg of the bi-pod leveling my crosshairs just over the bull's shoulder. The wind was blowing about 30 mph so I took into consideration the windage and slowly squeezed the trigger. The roar of the gun was followed by a deafening silence. In slow motion, I looked over the scope to look for my elk. He had fallen dead in his tracks never to rise again. My guide offered the reassuring words of "great shot!"

While the morning stars were fading, the sun peaked over the mountains welcoming the new day. I sat motionless and breathed deeply while soaking it all in. I was overcome with emotion to think I had just harvested my first elk. My thoughts momentarily drifted homeward as my heart filled with thanksgiving to my family for making the sacrifices needed for this trip. An hour later, I grabbed the rack of my first bull. What an awesome animal. Practice paid off!

In life, do you ever feel like you just can't get something right no matter how hard you try or how much you practice? Sometimes, I cry out, "Lord, how can I ever be righteous?" It seems no matter how hard I try I seem to fail. I just can't hit the target. Living a righteous life is a tough target. Truthfully, we can't hit the mark on our own. That's why I thank God for Jesus! He makes it possible to live a righteous life by living it *through* us.

Challenge: Are you falling repeatedly to a specific temptation? Do you feel trapped or ensnared by moral failure or impurity? Only Jesus, can set you free. Pray about it.

Thought: You can never manage sin for it will always master you.

> *But thanks be to God that though you were slaves of sin, you became obedient from the heart…and having been freed from sin, you became slaves of righteousness.* Romans 6:17-18

> *…who is able to do exceedingly abundantly beyond all we ask or think, according to the power that works within us…Amen.* Ephesians 3:20-21

Stay Alert

Silence can be a wonderful thing. Silence can be a deadly thing. Silence can be loud. Have you ever sat in a deer stand when Silence took over the microphone? You don't know whether he's screaming—"everybody stay in bed, its about to rain"—or "it's too hot, just wait till the moon rises before supper" or "intruder alert!" I'm not sure how to interpret Mr. Silence, but one thing is for sure—the inhabitants of the woods listen well.

On one such afternoon, I wasn't expecting to see any game. It was just too still for some reason. Using my tree-climbing stand, I jacked up a tree positioned between a honeysuckle thicket and creek bed. I kept reminding myself to "stay alert." About sunset, my eye caught movement to the left. As I slowly turned my head, I noticed a bobcat prowling silently along the thicket. I could hardly believe she was moving so quickly without making a sound. I thought to myself, "No wonder these cats are such efficient predators, they move with such grace and stealth."

I had set a goal earlier to harvest each of the predators in the South using my bow. So far, I had bagged a coyote and missed a red fox. I had not had an opportunity to take a gray fox. It now appeared I would have a chance to harvest my first bobcat with a bow. As the cat slowly and patiently approached my stand, she had no idea I was observing her. The cat jumped upon an old log to look around. I began to slowly draw my compound, but the cat caught my movement and looked up into the tree. I released the arrow and shot the cat directly in the heart. The cat let out a spine tingling scream and expired within a few seconds.

I was amazed at the beauty of this fine animal. Although I had caught bobcats in traps before, this one was different. There seemed to be a sort of mystique about her. I have always thought bobcats were the prettiest furbearers on the North American continent. I would certainly enjoy this one in my trophy room for years to come and the memory to go with it. But that is not all I gained from it.

I wondered what it would be like to have a real predator on *my* trail—a cougar, griz, or African lion—talk about a "spine tingling scream"—don't laugh. Many a grown man has screamed like a little girl while being pursued by one of these beasts. Fact is, if you knew one of these animals were on your trail, you *would* take it seriously. The Bible speaks of an adversary, an enemy, who prowls about like a lion looking for someone to devour. He moves gracefully and stealthily. This lion patiently stalks his prey. He longs to destroy you and is not in a hurry to do so. He is patient. The Word of God warns us to "be alert!"

Challenge: Do you take the devil as a *serious* threat to your life? He is a serious threat to you from Almighty God's perspective. Do *you* see him as such? The devil is out to destroy your life, family, and kids. He is a heartless liar. Stay alert!

Thought: To avoid becoming Satan's prey you must pray.

> *Be of sober spirit, be on the alert. Your adversary, the devil, prowls about like a roaring lion, seeking someone to devour.*   *1 Peter 5:8*

Life is Good

When I was a teenager, Daniel, Jonathan, and I decided to go rabbit hunting with our bows and arrows. In those days, virtually no one hunted small game with a bow. We carefully walked through the thickets maintaining a straight row with constant awareness of the others whereabouts. Hitting a moving target with a bow is a feat in itself—add to that the unpredictable hopping of Peter Cottontail and you have a challenge to say the least. Rabbits are always fun to hunt especially when there is plenty of action.

On this particular day, the little fuzz balls were running everywhere. We shot and shot. Judo points are wonderful for shooting at small game because they do not travel far when shot toward the ground. Several times our arrows barely missed the mark, but a *small* miss is still a miss nonetheless. Fortunately, the law of averages finally caught up with the rabbits. Suddenly, a cottontail broke out of a thicket in front of me and starting running across a low grass pasture. This gave time to draw my bow unhindered by brush or tree limbs. The bow swung smoothly as I caught up to the rabbit and released the arrow. The arrow hit the rabbit in the head and sent him into a complete somersault. He died immediately.

The field erupted with shouts and laughter as we cheered wildly coupled with "high fives" and hugs. You would have thought I killed a bull elephant with one arrow! We were ecstatic! We didn't realize how loud we actually were. Our neighbor came out of his house across the road wondering if someone had been hurt. When he discovered what had been accomplished, he smiled and said, "Just checking on you boys. Have fun."

It's been almost thirty years since that day and I can still remember it like it was yesterday. Oh, to be a kid again, with no care in the world—except hunting! I guess that's one reason why I enjoy hunting; it gives a man an opportunity to get away from it all. Sometimes the "all" follows us to the woods and makes it difficult to enjoy the hunt—things to do, unreturned phone calls, homework, and miscellaneous deadlines howl for us to turn around and "go to the house." The mental barrage battles hard to ruin the hunt and the relaxation we anticipated.

How did we *ever* get into such a stressful mess? Isn't time in the woods supposed to be fun? If so, then why do I sometimes feel guilty—like I am supposed to be somewhere else? How do I defeat this gnawing uneasiness? After all, didn't I come out here to have fun? Why am I anxious?

Challenge: Am I right with God? Am I right with my wife or have I acted selfishly pertaining to this hunt? Am I right with my fellow man? Why is my conscience bothering me? Is there a legitimate reason why my spirit is so uneasy? On the other hand, I may simply need to put the whining dogs of busyness at bay. My resolve may need to be—"Today, I will hunt and feel good about it. I will have fun! Tomorrow, I will finish the task at hand. Life is too short to work all the time—so today...I hunt!"

Thought: Selfishness does not make a good companion.

This is the day which the Lord has made, let us rejoice and be glad in it.   Psalm 118:24

Do not be anxious for tomorrow; for tomorrow will care for itself. Each day has enough trouble of it own.   Matthew 6:34

A Valuable Gift

Every man who has owned a hunting dog can testify to the closeness experienced between the hunter and his companion. Whether the dog is a setter, pointer, retriever, brit, beagle, redbone, or some other breed, hunting dogs are a lot of fun *if* they are well trained. Dogs can make you proud or really make you mad. My wife used to ask why my voice was hoarse when I came home from quail hunting. I usually retorted, "You wouldn't understand."

The dog will make or break your hunt. All things being said, there is nothing like watching a dog you have trained work a covey of quail, point a pheasant, or plunge into icy water to retrieve your prized canvasback. No sir, nothing like it. I guess you have to be a dog lover to understand.

At any rate, my first bird dog was an English Setter named Dan. He was a gift to me from a fellow hunter. I still remember teaching him to point a quail wing tied to an old cane fishing pole. As Dan's pointing instincts began to emerge, I would command, "Whoaaa, Dan…Whoaaa!" Hindsight tells me I should have worked harder on *this* command. It wasn't long before my puppy became a full-fledged hunting dog.

Years went by and due to Dan's good nose and some lucky shooting, many quail and woodcock filled our freezer. Ole Dan and I shared many memories together and sometimes we shared the hunt with a close friend or family member. Watching the sun rise across a frost covered bean field or watching the sun set beyond a patch of broom sedge awakens memories to this day of prickly briar thickets and the whir of the covey rise. Sometimes during the hunt, I wouldn't even shoot. I just enjoyed the sport.

One of my last memories of ole Dan occurred late one evening. Dan pointed a covey of quail and as the covey rose, I managed to get off a single shot. Dan quickly retrieved my bird and I headed for the truck since it was getting late. Dan came back a few minutes later with another bird in his mouth and took off again. Finally, he caught up with me at the truck with still another bird in his mouth. Apparently, I had killed three birds with one shot! This kind of thing makes you proud of your companion.

Ole Dan has been gone for a long time now. Presently, I do not own any hunting dogs. But the memories of my time with Dan are still very much alive. Sometimes, a gift can have more value than you realize. It can have a lifelong impact.

Challenge: Memories in the field are valuable gifts. Thank God for the memories and the people who help make them. Are you thankful for the gift of companionship? Tell your hunting buddies how much they mean to you. While there is still ample time, express to your wife and kids how much you enjoy sharing life with them.

Thoughts: If our relationships with animals can become so endearing, how much more important are our relationships with people and with God? The gift of companionship is a great gift indeed. Don't take it for granted.

> *If you then, being evil, know how to give good gifts to your children,*
> *how much more shall your heavenly Father who is in heaven give*
> *what is good to those who ask Him!* Matthew 7:11

Perfection

1994 proved to be a great year for me in terms of harvesting turkeys. I was privileged to hunt the Rio Grande in Texas and the Eastern Turkey in Alabama and Tennessee. During those years a hunter could harvest four turkeys in Tennessee but two of them had to come from management areas whose birds were included in the state bag limit. The season was coming to an end and I still had one tag left. However, I had to harvest my last bird on a management area. I had already killed six turkeys and really wanted to make it seven. The number seven is used symbolically in the Bible to represent completion or perfection. If I could finish the season harvesting seven birds, I would have a "perfect" season. I had one day left to accomplish this goal.

The following morning, I let out my best barred owl imitation. The echoing call was met with complete silence. I decided to sit and listen for the next hour. The sun was starting to rise when all of a sudden a single gobble occurred on top of the ridge directly above me. I gave the turkey time to fly down and crept up to his roost. I softly clucked and purred but to no avail. I decided to slowly move in the direction I thought the gobbler had pitched from the roost. As I listened intently, I heard the unmistakable sound of drumming…Pfttt Dmmmm…Pfttt Dmmmm that soon faded out of hearing. I moved another seventy-five yards and listened intently. Once again, I could hear that ole gobbler drumming…Pfttt Dmmmm…Pfttt Dmmmm. He would not respond to my softest calling techniques but continued drumming until I could hear him no longer. Then, I would move once again. This cat and mouse game continued until 11:30 a.m.

I wasn't sure exactly where the gobbler was, but I could still hear his drumming. "If he would only gobble one time," I thought to myself. About that time, an old truck came down the road about a quarter mile away. The truck had a chain in the back that rattled loudly as the vehicle bounced across several rough spots in the road. Ole tom couldn't stand this racket and let out a thunderous gobble. This was exactly the break I needed. I decided to either kill the turkey or scare him, but it was time to make a move. With gun shouldered, I slowly stood up behind a tree and saw the turkey about thirty-five yards away steadily strutting. He stepped behind a tree, giving me time to take off the safety and swing the gun.

The game had ended. What a hunt! This turkey had really gained my respect. Truthfully, it wouldn't have bothered me in the least if the outcome had been different. His tail fan hangs proudly displayed in my trophy room. Every time I look at it, I am reminded of that great hunt that ended the perfect season.

Challenge: Do you ever feel pressure to be perfect? I mean—do the job right—make the grades—don't get mad—don't be late—don't hold a grudge—never make mistakes. All of us face challenges to perform. Sometimes, we place stress on ourselves and raise a standard impossible to achieve. I'm glad that ultimately we only have to please one person—Jesus. He is fair in all of His judgments.

Thought: There was only one perfect being that walked the forest glades. The man who finds completion in Christ is sheltered against the battering waves of other's expectations. Do your best and leave the rest to God.

> *Therefore, you are to be perfect as your heavenly Father is perfect.*
> *Matthew 5:48*

The word "perfect" in this verse is literally translated "complete" or "whole." Our completeness doesn't come through perfect works but through a perfect God. Praise Him today for loving you despite your many flaws.

A Bird's Eye View

One gorgeous afternoon during the fall, I sat in my climbing stand waiting for whitetail deer that were slowly feeding in my direction. Purple flowers edged the field creating a beautiful backdrop for the unfolding hunt. Flocks of birds were busily looking for an afternoon snack. Robins, Starlings, Finches, and Wrens made up the fine feathered feeding frenzy.

I was distracted from my hunt by a number of smaller birds feeding beneath my stand and I quietly whispered a prayer, "Father, it sure would be neat if one of those little birds would fly up here and land on me." Much to my surprise, a few minutes later, something incredible happened. I was sitting with my recurve bow flat across my legs. An arrow was nocked and ready for the possible shot to come. All of a sudden, a little bird flies up and lands on my arrow shaft. He stays there for a few seconds and then lights on the left side of my bow and eventually lands on the right side of my bow. That little bird was all over me! I sat smirking to myself, "what will the guys think about this one?"

Better still, what was that little bird thinking? I figure the Lord had to be laughing at my response to the answered prayer. God answers our prayers. He is not sitting on a throne in heaven waiting to strike us with a lightening bolt if we get out of line. He is a caring and loving Father and wants the best for all of us. Everything created responds to His commands—everything except man.

God gives man a free choice to either live for himself or live in obedience to God. He knows if we live for ourselves we will eventually self-destruct. Alcohol, infidelity, greed, workaholism, addictions of all kinds, and misery begin to take their toll. Without God in our lives, inner peace is only something we imagine. God has provided a way for our lives to have deeper meaning and purpose. He truly wants us to be fulfilled, completed, and satisfied. Many think God only wants to take—when the truth is—Jesus came to give. The solution to the complex problems in life is really quite simple. Learn a lesson from the birds—obey God.

Challenge: If the birds obey His commands, how much more should we? If he cares for the birds, he will surely care for you. Birds never get lost and they always have a home. They never worry.

Thoughts: Are you willing to surrender the "small things" to God? *Everything* is "small" compared to His power. Is there anything you are worried about today? The next time you see the beautiful flowers and hear the songs of God's little birds, remember the following words of Jesus:

> *Are not two sparrows sold for a cent and yet not one of them will fall to the ground apart from your Father.*   Matthew 10:29

> *Look at the birds of the air, they do not sow, neither do they reap, nor gather into barns, and yet your heavenly Father feeds them. Are you not worth much more than they?*   Matthew 6:26

Trapped

Several years ago, I took my sons trapping. I have always been fascinated with trapping every since I saw my first mountain man movie. As
a teenager, I remember walking into a friend's fur shed. I was irrevocably
hooked. The hides of red foxes, coons, muskrats, mink, bobcats, and coyotes hung on each wall. Wow, I felt like I had died and entered Jeremiah
Johnson's heaven! I stayed in that fur shed for quiet some time brushing
the various furs and taking in all of the smells. Conibears, Victors, North
Woods, and an assorted variety of other traps littered the floor. Trap wax
and dye were sitting on the table and stakes, hammers, and shovels lay
beside the trapping basket. I made it a point to ask lots of questions and
my trapping career was launched that very day. Trapping always makes a
better hunter because it teaches the hunter to look for details that most
outdoorsmen simply miss. I dreamed of the days when I could take my
sons trapping.

Many years later, the day had arrived all too quickly. Previously, I made a
dirt hole fox set at the intersection of two old roads that coursed through
a cedar thicket. The following morning, my sons and I walked to the
site where the trap was set. As we neared the location of our fox set, it
became apparent that something was in the trap.

My youngest son, Reed, was four years old at the time and very inquisi-
tive about the creature jumping up and down in the trap. He looked in
wide-eyed wonder as he exclaimed, "Look at 'em daddy, he's dancing in
that trap...he's dancing in that trap!" Kids say the funniest things. I look
forward to the day when we can run a long trap line together.

Have you ever been so overjoyed that you felt like dancing? God has
made it possible through Jesus Christ to be ecstatically joyful. This
doesn't mean we will never experience problems or setbacks, but even in
the midst of defeat, we can still rejoice. Even though we may feel trapped

with nowhere to hide, we can leap for joy for Jesus has won the victory over our problems. The problem itself may not go away, but the way you view the problem changes everything.

Challenge: Are you facing dilemmas too big to handle? Do you feel trapped? Turn it over to God. Let *Him* take it from you. *He* can handle it. If severe consequences are on the way, He can strengthen you to get through them.

Thought: Nothing happens to us without first filtering through God's fingers.

You have turned for me my mourning into dancing.   Psalm 30:11

Hurts

I grew up in a small county seat town in Mississippi where there was a community park. This park had a small pond on the backside of the property. Like most ponds, there was always an abundance of small perch or bream to be caught. Additionally, every now and then, some local bass fisherman would release a bass or two into this pond. My friend, Tim, and I loved to ride our bicycles to this location and fish after school. On occasion we would meet an elderly black gentleman named Marvine. Marvine would always catch a few perch and every one of them no matter how small made it into his skillet. In keeping with our love for bream fishing, Tim and I started fly-fishing. We were introduced to this new method of fishing through a mutual friend of our parents.

We could hardly wait to get to the pond and try out our homemade flies and ants. It took several trips before we actually mastered the wrist action, but finally became fairly skilled with our new fly rods. The one thing that made the little pond such a good fly-fishing hole was the lack of trees around the edge. This gave us plenty of room to draw back and whip our flies wherever we wanted. We really didn't have to worry about what was behind us, because there was usually nothing to hang our hooks into.

One afternoon, ole Marvine showed up and was busy getting his tackle ready to fish. By this time, Tim had made it around the pond without realizing Marvine was behind him. Just about the time Marvine bent over to tie on his hook, Tim came back in one sweeping motion and landed his fly directly into Marvine's buttocks. As Tim's forward motion came to an abrupt halt, Marvine shouted, "Ooooooo, Ohhhhhh." Tim repentantly shouted, "Are you okay, Marvine? Are you okay?" Marvine shouted back, "Yes sir, I'm okay…me don't think it went to the bone!" Fortunately, the hook had completely ripped through a small section of Marvine's posterior and was lodged in his pants. After the initial surprise and realization that Marvine was okay, Tim and I were overcome with uncontrollable laughter.

Not many people would have responded like ole Marvine. In fact, some guys would have given us a thorough whippin' or a good cussin'. Marvine was a fine Christian gentleman who is now with Jesus. His gentleness and kindness toward two teenage boys impacts me to this day. Sometimes, we wound people not with actions but with our words. Although sometimes we may be kidding, words can quickly discourage the human spirit.

How do you respond when you see the look on the face of the one you have just wounded? Do you respond in self-justification or repentance?

Challenge: How do others view you? Do you build others up with words and actions or tear them down. Are you always in a bad mood and short tempered toward the people you love? Make a commitment today to surrender to the power of God's Holy Spirit. He alone can change your demeanor.

Thought: Careless words impact people for the rest of their lives— especially women and children.

For the mouth speaks out of that which fills the heart.

Matthew 12:34

The Tale of the Tail

Trot lining for catfish has always been one of my favorite outdoor activities. As a kid, we would stick cane poles into the bank of a creek. Lines tied to these poles would often be baited with crawfish or catalpa worms to create a sort of self-fishing system called a "bank hook." Each pole would be checked early in the morning to see if an unsuspecting cat was pulling on the pole. After receiving my driver's license, the bank hook quickly went the way of the dinosaur and was replaced by the age-old "trot line" (trout line).

There is nothing like a breezy ride up the river on a cold spring morning. The sun rises while patches of fog drift upward. It is always a relief to reach your trotlines so your teeth can stop chattering! Then, there are those pleasant evenings when the sun is setting, your lines are set, and you're headed for the boat ramp. Owls fly across the river retreating from the humming outboard while bats dart here and there catching mosquitoes. The shadows of cypress trees draped with Spanish moss gives the entire area a kind of mysterious wildness. If your lucky, you get back to the ramp without hitting any submerged logs and only a few bugs to clean from your eyes or face. Life is good! The next morning, you are filled with anticipation as you approach the first line.

On one such morning, I landed a thirty-pound "yellow cat" (appaloosa, tabby, flathead, etc.). He was a nice fish to say the least. However, while running the next line, I could feel something very large on the line. Since I was fishing in deep water and baited with bluegill, I guessed the fish to be another big yellow cat. The fish swam along the bottom for a long time. I was very careful to avoid the empty hooks on the trotline should the fish surge in an effort to get away. A fish this big can be very dangerous. I gently pulled on the fish for fifteen minutes and never got him off the bottom. Eventually, my stainless steel hook popped loose. As the line slipped through my fingers, I knew he had gotten away.

The hook was completely straightened when I pulled the line into the boat. I commented to my friend, Justin, "Man, I wonder how big that one was?" I could tell by the sheer weight of the fish and the way he was swimming that he was a huge cat. Although I couldn't see the bottom in fifty feet of water, I was sure this cat was as big as my boat. I could feel his tail rocking his body to and fro. I was sure he was the fish of a life-time—80, 90, 100 pounds and he got away! He probably wasn't as big as I thought he was—but so it goes with fishing stories. I will never know.

Challenge: Do you live in constant regret because something "big" just slipped through your fingers and got away—maybe a business deal, piece of property, championship game, or broken relationship? Sometimes these kinds of things can rob our joy and gnaw away the quality of our lives.

Thoughts: When something really gets to you, ask the question: "What difference is this going to make tomorrow or next week?" Many times, the answer reveals the issue is not as big as you think. Don't imagine the situation to be bigger than it is. Besides, God is absolutely sovereign in *all* things. He is in control. Are you willing to trust Him? This is an opportunity for God to show you how big *He* really is. And that's no tale. It's a fact.

> *And we know that God causes all things to work together for good to those who love God, to those who are called according to His purpose.*   Romans 8:28

Be Careful Where You Sit

Some time ago, a friend of mine, Cliff Forbis, was turkey hunting in Tennessee. After getting up early, driving an hour and climbing up and down hardwood hills and hollers, he sensed it was time for a siesta. Often, this is what your body beckons as the sun warms up the cool spring air and a gentle spring breeze greets the morning. On such an occasion, Cliff had been hunting for several hours and decided to take a short nap. He found a large beech tree and decided to park himself at its base. As he leaned back against the tree, he nodded into a deep sleep. Without realizing it, Cliff had sat in front of a small hole located at the base of the tree. No, we are not talking about yellow jacket wasps but something much worse.

Within half an hour, my friend was awakened to the sound of dry leaves cracking. You know, that sound a turtle makes as he pushes his shell along the forest's floor or the sound a snake makes when slithering through the leaves. King snakes, black snakes, rat snakes, are no problem. Only this sound was not being made by one of these.

Cliff awakened to realize a large rattlesnake was crawling toward his groin. The snake was still several feet away. Cliff was completely startled as the snake slowly came into focus by his previously sleepy eyes. Now wide awake—Cliff reached for his gun. The snake immediately coiled and began to rattle furiously. Fortunately, Cliff was able to fire between his legs and dispatch the snake immediately. In his own words, "I blew that pile of rattlesnake everywhere!" (I imagine that wasn't the only "pile" he left beside that ole beech.)

As one can imagine, he later told me, that experience ruined his entire hunt. From that moment forward, every stick and branch was a danger-ous threat. Every dirt hole was potentially fatal and every creature crawl-ing across the leaves was out to get him. "I don't know if I will ever get over it," he later admitted. "One thing is for sure," he commented. "I was out of the woods before dark—that snake almost made me quit turkey hunting for good."

Challenge: Have you ever been so rattled by something in your past that you couldn't move ahead into the future without constant fear? You simply don't feel like you will *ever* get over it. God's grace enables us to overcome "the past" (no matter what has happened). Sometimes things happen *to* us or *through* us. Either way, God makes all things new. He can even make *people* new. Don't park your life next to your fears or failures. Move on!

Thought: Although you may feel like quitting this grand adventure called life, you don't have to stay where you are. Everyone and everything is *not* out to get you. Move away from a negative attitude and life perspective. Rise up and walk!

> *Therefore, if any man is in Christ, he is a new creature; the old things passed away; behold, new things have come.*
>
> 2 Corinthians 5:17

> *Arise, take up your pallet and walk.*   John 5:8

Where the Blood Falls

Louisiana, "Sportsman's Paradise" read the tag on the slowly passing vehicle. I could hardly wait to get there. I was on my way to visit a long-time friend and boyhood companion, Roger Tanner, for a three-day bow hunt in northern Louisiana. Roger had harvested some nice whitetails over the years. Needless to say, I was excited that he had invited me to share in a few hunts. The stands were already in place. The only problem was I had to do a lot of climbing on this particular hunt. I had to climb out of bed, into the truck, off the four-wheeler, and up the tree. Boy, talk about an easy hunt. Roger had really gone out of his way to make this an enjoyable experience.

The first few hours on the stand, I saw numerous does and a small buck. Since we were not trophy hunting, any deer would be fair game. However, none had come within comfortable shooting distance. About 9:30 a.m. a small buck appeared and was moving away from my stand. I had a good quartering away shot at twenty yards and decided to take the shot. The arrow flew true to aim and the buck crashed out of sight. An hour later, Roger showed up and we began the tracking process.

I am red color deficient and this makes tracking a real job. What other hunters can see easily, takes great effort on my part. I must track extremely slowly to follow a blood trail and many times get down on my hands and knees to see any blood at all. Others without my handicap can walk slowly and never stop as they follow a "good blood trail."

On this particular occasion, I was thankful Roger was trailing with me. Roger was walking in front as I followed behind. Suddenly, he abruptly stopped and put his hand behind him causing me to stop as well. He slowly backed up. Then, he said, "look right there." As my eyes focused on the trail, I noticed a copperhead fully coiled. He had several drops of bright red blood on his back! Evidently, my deer had walked or jumped directly over the snake and left this vile creature covered with his blood. After killing the snake, we soon recovered my young buck. Roger and I sat and admired the plumpness of the young three pointer. We had a great hunt those next few days and arrowed several other deer. But our conversation kept turning to the blood-covered snake.

Challenge: Details in life are important. If you don't believe that, then just ask a woman! Many times men miss the most basic details. The *most* important detail to recognize is our need for cleansing. Sometimes, we need help tracking along the path of life—someone needs to point out the blood. Only the blood of Jesus can cleanse us from the vileness of sin. People can be quite venomous at times, especially with our words and actions. We deserve death as a consequence to the deadly poison we sometimes spread.

Thoughts: The blood of Jesus can cleanse the vilest person. I thank God His precious blood has covered me. Are you covered by His blood?

> *All of us like sheep have gone astray, each of us has turned his own way; But the Lord has caused the iniquity of us all to fall on Him.*
> Isaiah 53:6

> *In Him we have redemption through His blood, the forgiveness of our trespasses...*
> Ephesians 1:7

Legacy

Late one evening, I managed to roost a small flock of turkeys near the top of a ridge. I literally saw them fly up. The next morning, I made my way to the area where the birds were located. They were nowhere to be found. I was positively in the correct place. It was pitch black when I left the roost and pitch black when I arrived the next morning. The previous night was met with violent thunderstorms, wind, and rain and the only thing I could figure was they changed trees during the night. At any rate, the turkeys were nowhere to be found and did not gobble to reveal their new location.

I continued searching that morning by setting up at various locations and "blind calling." I simply hoped to run across an ole gobbler by sitting down at "the right place at the right time." During my third setup, I was sitting with my back next to a tree. Out in front of me, I noticed some mushrooms shaped in a peculiar fashion. After sitting approximately twenty minutes, I got up for a closer look at the mushrooms. They were not mushrooms at all, but two finely polished antlers from a young eight-point buck. A beautiful set indeed—four symmetrical points on each side. I started thinking how unusual it was to find both sides together. I love to discover antler sheds, although I am not the luckiest person when it comes to actually finding them. I couldn't help but wonder what the buck was doing at that moment or where he might be. What would he look like next year? Would he still be around this area during next hunting season? Funny how things left behind can foster so many questions.

I have several "keepsakes" left behind by friends who are no longer with us. They remind me of the people who gave them. One such keepsake is a slate call given to my son by the late Jerry Turner. Jerry was a co-worker with Harold Knight and David Hale of Knight and Hale Game Calls, Inc. Jerry courageously fought cancer for many months, but eventually died a few years ago. He was a champion in life and the best turkey hunter a man could ever wish to meet. He taught me a lot and I think of him each spring. After Jerry's funeral, Harold Knight came up to me and made this statement, "Jerry not only showed us how to live, but he showed us how a man is supposed to die." I will never forget those words. Jerry Turner left behind an eternal legacy.

Challenge: Are you building a lasting legacy of honesty, integrity, truth, unselfishness, and eternal focus? Are you so consumed with the pressures of the next business deal or overly booked schedule that you are forgetting the real reason we live? How long has it been since you really focused on the needs of your children or wife—without being distracted? What will their thoughts be of you when they discover the things you have left behind? What kinds of questions will they ask?

Thoughts: The value of a man's life is not determined by the things he accumulates, but by the real treasure he leaves behind—his investment in *people.* I once knew a man who left behind a string of antlers but a very unsettled family. Watching them cope with their loss was sad indeed. Through the years, that man has served as a prime example to me of a fine hunter who left behind the wrong treasures.

> *Do not lay up for yourselves treasures upon earth, where moth and rust destroy, and where thieves break in and steal. But lay up for yourselves treasures in heaven, where neither moth nor rust destroys, and where thieves do not break in and steal. For where your treasure is, there your heart will be also.* Matthew 6:19-21

Smokey the Bandit

When I was a young man, I lived in southern Mississippi. The swamps of the deep South were always filled with critters—including mosquitoes! I remember being unable to hunt several afternoons due to the hordes of mosquitoes trying to munch on my torso. It was miserable! I always looked forward to the approaching cooler weather when the mosquitoes would be elsewhere. During the winter, I would often set a trap line of several hundred traps. It wasn't long before the fur began to pile up—coon, muskrat, nutria, mink, fox, coyote, and bobcat filled my wire stretchers. There's nothing like a shed filled with fur.

This particular year, I would take my canoe and run about 50 sets in the swamp before checking another 150 land sets. I loved paddling along the sloughs observing the old Spanish moss hanging from massive cypress trees. While running my sets, my mind often drifted to an era when life was much more difficult—to a time when early trappers settled this difficult land. Did one of them actually trap this same line? What were their names? Did they ever get discouraged or tip over their canoe? My thoughts were interrupted as I paddled quietly around a bend in the slough. Wood ducks squealed in retreat as they headed for another secluded waterway and I couldn't help but reflect on the reasons I loved the swamp.

As my canoe cut through the glazed surface of the water, I could see my intended destination—a large cypress. I had placed the trap between a cypress knee at the base of the tree and the tree itself. Coons were regularly walking between these two natural barriers. As I glided toward the set location, it was apparent a coon was in the trap. However, something looked strangely out of place. I couldn't believe my eyes. The coon was smoking a cigarette! Yep, that's right. I would have given anything to have my camera! As I neared the coon, it became apparent the coon was not actually smoking a cig. He had been chewing on the big cypress tree and a long white piece of bark was sticking out of his mouth. The early morning fog rising behind the animal looked exactly like smoke. I *still* wish I had my camera. It looked *exactly* like a cigarette. Even though my mind kept telling me, "Coons don't smoke"—my eyes were telling me, "Oh, yes they do—I see 'em!" That day, I learned a lesson in life from that old coon. Things are not always as they appear to be.

Challenge: Do you make judgments concerning others simply from the way things appear to be? Are you quick to form opinions before you have all of the facts? There is always "another side of the coin." Don't be too quick to make judgments concerning others. Just because you think you see smoke doesn't mean there is fire.

Thoughts: Sometimes professing Christians are the worlds worst at judging others. We immediately believe what we hear instead of giving the accused an opportunity to share their side of the story. Sometimes, we need to ignore the story altogether.

> *Do not judge lest you be judged. For in the way you judge, you will be judged; and by your standard of measure, it will be measured to you.*
> *Matthew 7:1-2*

Misses

How can we tell stories about our hunting adventures and never talk about the stalks we've blown or the "all-out misses?" Wouldn't it be great if the word "miss" wasn't in the dictionary? Then, we could just say (with integrity), "I...I...I don't know what happened." How many times have I heard (and stated) the old saga, "I can't believe I missed him" (or some derivative thereof)? Countless—countless times I have heard this statement. I missssed! Hard for that word to roll from our lips isn't it? Yet, the fact is some hunting camps have more shirttails nailed to the side of the clubhouse than siding. All of us miss from time to time—*all* of us.

Sometimes we get too serious about the hunt and can no longer laugh with one another. Ever had a covey rise in a wide-open field and miss every one of them? How about a flock of ducks landing right in the middle of your decoys—missed 'em all! Have you ever had an "easy" ten yard bow shot and completely missed (be honest on this one)? How about the turkey that walked right up to you—you emptied your gun only to watch him fly away unscathed. Remember him? Occasionally, *all* of us miss. Once you stop crying, it's easy to laugh. Maybe we need to stop laughing at each other and start crying with each other. Hunting is not about harvesting, bragging, numbers, or commercialization.

It is amazing how many of us place our identity in "success." Our entire identity can be falsely based on how others see us in terms of our hunting "success." I have watched full grown men strut around as if they are really the Big Cheese because they happened to be in the right place at the right time and killed (or paid an exorbitant amount of money for) a big whitetail. Those individuals who bag trophy bucks in fair chase settings on a regular basis deserve our respect and admiration. But let's remember that this is a sport we are talking about and our country has deified sports of all kinds. Just because a man is a great turkey hunter or bags multiple big bucks doesn't make him a better husband or father to his children. Neither does it mean he is a success in his job or other undertakings. On the contrary, many of these same guys have sacrificed much in their interpersonal relationships to be "successful" and well thought of by their peers.

No, I am not jealous. I am simply truthful and realistic. Many of these huge bucks we see in the magazines are grown on game farms and sometimes the hunters pictured with such animals did not even kill them. They are simply advertising a product. Many great hunters do not live in areas of the country where big whitetails are grown. Consequently, they can hunt an entire lifetime and perhaps never see a buck scoring more than 150 Boone and Crocket points. Are they any less a hunter for this fact? I think not. Many people are judging our outdoor sport by the wrong criteria.

Hunting is about companionship and camaraderie. Hunting is about relaxation and reflection. Don't get me wrong. I love to experience the thrill of the harvest and the good table fare that goes with it. But the goal of "successful" hunting should not be our god and the constant preoccupation with hunting success should not master our lives. Furthermore, this "success" should not determine the measure of our manhood.

Challenge: Do you spend every free moment thinking of next hunting season? When you mention "next year" does your wife roll her eyes? Do your kids beg you to stay home? If you answered, "yes" to these questions, your obsession with hunting has gotten out of balance. Talk to your family and find a balance in meeting your needs and theirs. Don't miss your time with them. You only get one opportunity with family. Start today and make your best shot count!

Thought: You can spend your entire life in self-indulgence and miss the things that really matter—*people*. Christ alone should master our lives.

Brethren, I do not regard myself as having laid hold of it yet; but one thing I do: forgetting what lies behind and reaching forward to what lies ahead, I press on toward the goal for the prize of the upward call of God in Christ Jesus.   Philippians 3:13-14

Snake Handlers

When I was in college, I spent a fair amount of time hunting. I guess I should have been in class, but the call of the wild was louder than the ring of the tardy bell. Besides, studying from a tree stand can be just as productive as the library (minus the girls). Although Saturday nights may have been a little lonely, mornings in the woods more than made up for it. One of my favorite places to hunt was a place called Cedar Creek Road. I enjoyed bow hunting along a particular bean field at the end of the road. On this particularly dry October morning, I was leaving the stand to walk back to my vehicle. I saw something moving in the road and just happened to notice it had an arrowhead shaped head. I slowly nocked and arrow and drew my bow. Three shots later, I had killed my first rattlesnake with a bow. He was not exceptionally large but a nice size snake (if there is such a thing)—he had eight rattles.

I started thinking how cool it would be to clean this snake and carry him back to the dorm for a snake fry. Yep, the guys at the dorm would think I was Daniel Boone with this one. Besides, everyone knows what a delicacy rattlesnake is. Right? Rattlesnake is the prettiest white meat you will ever see. After skinning the snake, I promptly placed him in a plastic bag in the small freezer compartment of our rental fridge. Weeks went by and we often talked about cooking "the snake" but never managed to find the time to do it. Before we knew it, Christmas break rolled around and it was time to go home for a few weeks. Unbeknownst to me, in an effort to save electricity, my roommate opened the fridge and checked for food but did not check the freezer. After which, he thoughtfully unplugged the unit.

About a month later, we returned from Christmas break and were forced to place the fridge outside our dorm room. I had smelled many rotten things before, but rotten rattlesnake was not among them. To this day, the thought of it still makes me grimace. What putrid stench! Our entire room had to be de-fumigated. This raunchy smell wafted into the hall-way where others shared their opinions as well. Our small rental fridge sat alone, outside, for an entire semester. No one stole the unit (can't imagine why). The outside looked fine—it was the inside that hid the problem. Finally, I had to scrub it with bleach, soap, and water before returning it to the rental location. The bleach gave the once discolored unit a clear appearance.

The Bible explains how vile and putrid our sin is before God and that it not only affects us, but all those around us. Sin destroys us from the inside out. Even when you become accustomed to the decay within, others can clearly see a life marked by bad decisions, self-indulgence, and selfishness. Thank God, Jesus came to deliver us from such an empty scarred existence.

Challenge: Is there a specific sin in your life that needs to be con-fessed and brought under the blood of Jesus? His blood is the only thing that can make you clean again. He not only cleanses us but also gives us the power to stay clean. Does your family or friends constantly remind you of the wreaking presence of sin in your life? What have you done about it? The next time you smell something rotting on the side of the road, praise the Lord He has cleansed you from the stench of sin.

Thoughts: Without the power of Christ, your life will decay from *within*. It doesn't matter how good you think you are, you still need cleansing from the inside out—and this is a daily process.

> Now the deeds of the flesh are evident, which are: immorality, impu-rity, sensuality, idolatry, sorcery, enmities, strife, jealousy, outbursts of anger, disputes, dissensions, factions, envying, drunkenness, carousing, and things like these, of which I forewarn you just as I have forewarned you that those who practice such things shall not inherit the kingdom of God. But the fruit of the Spirit is love, joy, peace, patience, kindness, goodness, faithfulness, gentleness, self-control; against such things there is no law. Now those who belong

to Christ Jesus have crucified the flesh with its passions and desires.
If we live by the Spirit, let us also walk by the Spirit.

Galatians 5:19-25

And you were dead in your trespasses, in which you formerly
walked according to the course of this world, according to the prince
of the power of the air, of the spirit that is now working in the sons
of disobedience. Among them we too all formerly lived in the lusts
of our flesh, indulging the desires of the flesh and of the mind,
and were by nature children of wrath, even as the rest, But God,
being rich in mercy, because of His great love with which He loved
us, even when we were dead in our transgressions, made us alive
together with Christ and raised us up with Him, and seated us with
Him in the heavenly places, in Christ Jesus…   *Ephesians 2:1-6*

Seasons of Reflection

The Smallness of Man

I was hunting for whitetails along a heavily wooded ridge. It was a frigid morning with temperatures dropping into the teens. My entire body was almost numb. Several days earlier, I had located a persimmon thicket at the end of a long ridge. Deer droppings where everywhere and I knew this would be a good place to connect. Therefore, I strategically placed my stand downwind of the expected ambush point.

Just about the time the sun was coming up, I noticed a nice buck coming into view. The buck was traveling directly from the east, which made me look directly into the sun as he was approaching. The glare from the sun made it difficult to see through my scope at the intended target. However, when he walked in front of a tree, I could see clearly and managed to squeeze off a shot. The buck immediately bolted off the ridge toward the creek bottom below.

I am red-green color deficient and it is very difficult to trail a deer. However, with patience and persistence, I can usually follow the trail. I started looking for blood and couldn't find any at first. Then, I began seeing fresh blood on the leaves and followed it in the bright sunshine. The trail started out okay but then began to sporadically weave to and fro. Again, I was looking directly into the rising sun and the glare was intense. I knew the immediate direction the buck had bolted and the trail didn't make sense.

Surprisingly, I felt something running down my nose. It was too cold and too soon into the tracking process to be sweat. As I felt the bridge of my nose, I noticed blood on my finger. I was confused for a brief moment and then I realized what had happened. When aiming at the buck, I had compensated for the sun's glare in my scope by sighting too closely to the scope's eye guard. My expected eye relief was eliminated. Apparently, the recoil from the gun caused the scope to cut my forehead between the eyes. Due to the brightness of the sun and difficulty with my vision I had not realized I had been tracking myself! It took about thirty seconds to come to this realization. I would have laughed at myself, but at the time, it wasn't funny.

I retraced my steps to the original position where the deer was hit and began following the *real* trail. Several minutes later, I was standing beside my buck. I took care of my prize and decided to continue hunting since I still had a doe permit in my pocket. I did not see another deer all day until late in the evening. This time the lighting conditions were very low. I could see clearly through my scope but it was getting almost too dark for a safe shot.

I was leaving the woods when all of a sudden a big doe started walking on a trail broadside to me. Since the light was fading, I unconsciously placed the scope closer to my eyes than usual. After the shot, I felt a hot liquid running down my nose (Yes sir, did it again…twice in one day…that's got to be a record for complete stupidity. "What an idiot," I thought to myself, "I cannot believe you did this again" ("you" of course, referring to the scope).

At any rate, maybe it wouldn't look that bad or maybe the cuts would run together so there wouldn't be the tale-tale mark of twice an idiot. I continued to chastise myself for being the dumbest human on the planet. My forehead looked pretty bad, but I thought it was going to be okay.

My wife and kids sympathetically ooed and aahed before they broke into a restrained sort of laughter. At least they tried and this gave me an indication of how others would respond to my story. Maybe, I could somehow keep it a secret. What would I say when people asked? And they *would* ask.

That evening, we decided to eat supper at our local fish restaurant. As we entered the restaurant, I was hoping no one would notice the gaping wounds between my eyes. This was embarrassing for a "seasoned" hunter like myself. After the hostess seated us, I noticed a man across the aisle with an orange hat on his head. Oddly enough, he had a big cut upon his forehead right between his eyes. Our eyes met simultaneously, in complete disbelief he stared at me and I stared at him. Seconds turned into what seemed like hours. Finally, I broke the silence and pointed to my forehead and laughingly said, "The sun sure was bright this morning wasn't it?" He just laughed and shook his head—we didn't have to say another word.

Challenge: How's your self-esteem? Sometimes we beat ourselves up for the smallest mistakes. Truth is—most of us take our hunting very seriously. Occasionally, stupid things happen to all of us. Have you ever tripped and fallen on your face while hunting or slipped into a creek? These kinds of things remind us not to take ourselves too seriously. There is more to live for than maintaining our prideful demeanor of boastfulness and pretending our hunts always turn out perfectly.

Thoughts: Do you live for anything bigger than yourself? Someone once said the smallest package in the world is a man wrapped up in himself.

> *…for everyone who exalts himself shall be humbled, but he who humbles himself shall be exalted.* Luke 18:14

> *Humble yourselves in the presence of the Lord, and He will exalt you.* James 4:10

Trophies

I have always been fascinated with trophies. I guess it all started when I was a little boy playing peewee football and baseball. This Indiana Jones pursuit of treasure kept me busy throughout high school. Winning a trophy or plaque represented a crowning achievement. After graduating from high school there was no one to catch the touchdown pass. There was no one to keep score. Therefore, my complete focus became the competition between the quarry hunted and myself.

I always enjoyed hunting more than athletics anyway. My frenzied behavior gave the greatest satisfaction—facing game on its turf where *I* had the disadvantage. It all became an extension of the competition I experienced in high school and quite predictably became an obsession. It is easy to justify obsessions because they completely dominate our thoughts. Every spare moment was occupied by hunting magazines and videos. During social events, I was always looking for my fellow hunters so we could strike up a conversation about hunting. My wife and I managed to navigate many—shall we say, "tense"—discussions concerning my love for hunting.

Years passed and children came on the scene demanding even more of my time. As my career advanced, more of my time was required. I tried to maintain my constant pursuit of animals as much as possible as hunting continued to be my first love when it came to recreation. Time passed and I managed to collect quite a few nice trophies.

Entering into my mid-thirties, I began to see life through a completely new set of lenses. One day I realized how many of us actually worship deer antlers, turkey beards, and large fish. We would not call it "worship" but that is exactly what it is—our desire to attain these things consumes every free moment. Bone, feathers, and scales is what it boils down to. My life was being spent in pursuit of bone, feathers, and scales to the exclusion of all else. Human relationships, family vacations, and the needs of others in life, all took a backseat to my pursuit of the big three. I'm glad I finally came to myself and realized what was happening. I still hunt a great deal, but not at the sacrifice of the things that are most important—namely my wife and children.

I schedule a family vacation during the kids' spring break (which just happens to be during the peak period of turkey season!) and always check the family calendar before planning hunting trips. This keeps me from missing important events with my kids at school. Additionally, I am attempting to provide my wife as much money to spend on her hobbies as I spend on mine. This is only fair. No, I do not have as many days in the field as I did in the days before I grew up. Interestingly enough, I still bag as many turkeys and deer as I always did and my days afield are more enjoyable since I am not at odds with my wife. All in all, I am enjoying my outdoor experiences more now than ever before.

My kids are getting old enough to hunt and now my trophies are different than before. The real trophy is to see the look on the face of my kids when they kill their first deer or turkey. How wonderful it is to hear my son say, "Dad, can I get him mounted?" These are the trophies that last—unforgettable moments shared with children. Teaching the next generation about hunter ethics, the sport of the hunt, and the God who created it all are the trophies I now pursue. Don't get my wrong, I am still a serious outdoorsman who loves to kill a nice buck, turkey, or catch a large bass. It's just my life is more balanced than before. Balance in life is the key to ultimate enjoyment of the outdoor experience. I guess you could say my definition of *trophy* has changed.

Challenge: Do you pursue *your* love for the outdoors at the expense of all other relationships? Have you made a god out of selfish ambition and personal goals? Are you keeping your life balanced when it comes to recreation? How do you define the term trophy?

Thought: When you stand before God and lay your "trophies" at His feet, will your accomplishments in life only consist of bone, feathers, and scales?

> *For where your treasure is there your heart will be also.*
>
> *Matthew 6:21*

Ode to Fred

Fred was one of those turkeys I just couldn't seem to catch in the right place at the wrong time (for him, that is). He would always shut up and quietly slip away without giving away his intended direction of travel. I had hunted Fred for three years and never seen him, but only heard his gobbles. I gave this turkey a name because he had eluded me for three seasons and he deserved respect on a higher level than any normal tom. On this particular hunt, my nine-year-old son, Grant, and I were camping. While we were cooking breakfast, a turkey started gobbling on an adjacent ridge. We were camped in a small field surrounded by hardwood ridges.

We quickly crammed down our remaining breakfast and headed for the gobbling bird. By the time we reached him, he stopped gobbling. I believe someone else heard him announcing his location to the world and bumped him from the roost. At any rate, no sooner had we made it to our destination that ole Fred started gobbling from the same ridge were he usually roosted. Fred gobbled his customary three times and shut up. I had to make a decision. The terrain was very steep and the weather was threatening rain. Additionally, I had this young boy in tow. Would he be able to make the trek?

I almost dismissed the notion to pursue Fred because I knew in addition to the difficult terrain and threatening weather, he would be difficult to kill. After all, I had chased ole Fred many times and knew he was a smart old bird. Against the odds for a successful hunt, Grant and I decided to make our way to Fred's location. We climbed back down the mountain and headed toward our camp on the adjacent side. As we neared camp, it started raining and Grant decided to go back to sleep and crawled back into the tent. I hurried toward the last place Fred had gobbled and made several soft calls. Much to my surprise in the light drizzle, Fred answered my calls with a hardy gobble. He kept moving and I kept following.

Interestingly enough, Fred made a large circle and marched right through the middle of our camp steadily gobbling. Grant was apparently asleep.

After about an hour and a half of this hide and seek game, Fred started moving steadily away. He was doing it again. I made a decision to either kill Fred or scare the tail feathers out of him. I was not going to allow this bird to walk away and forget our dialogue. I knew I needed to hurry if I was going to catch a glimpse of this worthy adversary. The last time he gobbled he was headed down the side of the mountain. As best as I could estimate, Fred was about thirty yards down the slope with a big red oak between us. This red oak forked about four feet up the truck. I quickly devised a plan to hurriedly ease up behind the oak and peer between the trunks looking for Fred. Past experience had taught me to raise my gun first and look for the turkey as I aimed my shotgun. I had allowed more than one gobbler to get away by trying to see him first and then get my gun up.

As I slowly raised my gun while looking between the forks of the red oak, I could see Fred in a half strut down the side of the mountain. I spoke out loud, "It's over now, Fred." Immediately, Fred raised his head and I pulled the trigger. Fred had finally been outwitted. One thing is for sure. Fred was a "runner" and he was highly unlikely to come blindly to a call. I felt a great sense of accomplishment to finally bag this bird. Back at camp, my son and I exchanged pats on the back as we relived the hunt. I am forever glad I decided to pursue Fred one more time. Fred sported sharp, curved spurs telling the tale of at least four seasons. Throwing Fred over one's shoulder would have been a delight to any turkey hunter. Grant and I quickly broke camp, loaded our gear onto the four-wheeler, and headed home in the rain. What a great memory. Once again, my resolve to "kill him or scare him," had paid off. The weather was terrible, the terrain steep, and the adversary difficult, but I was glad I had not given up on the hunt.

Challenge: Are you a quitter? Do you easily give up when things get tough? What are you struggling with right now that makes you want to throw up your hands and quit? Are you tempted to give up on your marriage, children, or career? Things may look bleak and the hill may seem too steep to climb. Will your children make the climb? Against the odds, what is your resolve?

Thoughts: We are not governed by odds or fate, but the sovereign will of God. God has a purpose for your circumstances. The most valuable things in life are worth your perseverance in faith. Don't give up!

I have fought the good fight, I have finished the course, I have kept the faith.   *2 Timothy 4:7*

Seasons of Reflection

You Never Know

I have always loved to catch bluegill bream. Ounce per ounce these pan fish can hold their own when it comes to fighting. Many years ago, I was fishing in Louisiana with a dear friend of mine, Roger Tanner. We rigged our cane poles with twelve-pound tests, quills, small split shots, and worms. Fishing among the lily pads has always been fun to me. You never know what will grab your bait and take off. Big bream usually don't mess around much but take your bait extremely fast. I guess that is how they get so big—they beat the other fish to the plate.

There has always been something mysterious about fishing in Louisiana. The big cypress trees draped with Spanish moss combined with the rising early morning fog give the bayou a sort of prehistoric appearance. On this particular morning, we had caught quite a few bream and were having a great day. Suddenly, I looked to my right and noticed a large alligator rising silently beneath our boat to the surface of the water. This reptile was longer than our fourteen-foot boat and deserved the respect we gave him as we slowly paddled away. I was glad to be in the boat instead of the water.

From that point on, I wished for a trolling motor instead of a paddle. I was glad to be in the boat with someone who had navigated these waters before. After seeing the big gator, there was something about scuttling the boat with half of my arm dangling over the water that gave me the creeps. Nevertheless, we continued to fish and fill our cooler with bluegill (this was before daily limits were set on this particular lake).

About ten o'clock in the morning, we were fishing by some small cypress trees when all of a sudden the most awful racket I have ever heard echoed from the top of the trees. A blackbird had been caught by a water moccasin and was squawking as loud as possible doing his best to get away. By this time, the snake had the upper hand and pulled the blackbird out of the tree. The snake fell fifteen to twenty feet from the top of the tree with blackbird in tow. They both hit the water with a splash only a few feet from the boat. The only thing left of Mr. Blackbird were bubbles and the silent witness of feathers wafting slowly to the surface of the water. This was the only time in my life I had seen such random wildness. Of course, when you fish in the bayous of Louisiana, you never know what to expect.

Challenge: How many people do you know who never lived a full life or died prematurely? Are you living today as if it were your last day? Is your house in order? Is there anyone you need to make amends with today? You never know what to expect in life. Death continually stalks every one of us and eventually catches us. There are no exceptions.

Thought: When you are in the boat with Jesus, you don't have to worry what is perched above or lurking below. He has navigated these waters before. You are safe with Jesus.

> *Therefore do not be anxious for tomorrow for tomorrow will care for itself. Each day has enough trouble of its own.*   Matthew 6:34

Green Horns

I guess the first time I heard the word "Green Horn" was in the movie "Jeremiah Johnson." Robert Redford played the part of a young man trying to live in the high country as a mountain man. He would have starved to death his first winter had it not been for an old-timer trapper and an empathetic Indian. Jeremiah (Redford) eventually learned how to survive in the mountains and how to avoid being scalped.

I had three sisters growing up and my oldest sister seemed to date guys who were always Green Horns when it came to the great outdoors. Sooner or later, they would get around to asking about my hunting experiences and invariably wanted to join me on a hunt. Since these guys were each my potential brothers-in-law, I wanted to show them a good time and test their mettle in the great outdoors.

One particular duck hunt, my sister's boyfriend borrowed my dad's waders. It needs to be said, this was before the days of neoprene waders. Waders in those days were made of rubber—big—awkward—and dangerous. I had been killing quite a few ducks on a particular slough and decided this would be a good place to try out my new friend. As we arrived at the intended destination, I asked Harv (names have been changed to protect the guilty) to "stand over there in that opening." Now, if you are smirking about now, it is only because you know what's coming. And you only know what's coming because you have done this before.

Honestly, I liked the guy. I was merely trying to position him where he could have an open shot at the ducks when they passed overhead. Besides, the water was only knee deep and this guy was in college. It never entered my mind to ask *why* there was such an opening in flooded timber. But it didn't take long to find out. I heard a loud splashing sound and looked over in the direction where Harv was settling in for the hunt. All I could see was Harv's hat floating on the water. Now, please understand, at the time, this wasn't funny at all. I mean, what was my sister going to say when I returned to tell her I had lost Harv and couldn't find anything but his hat? Suddenly, up he came gasping for air. I immediately helped him regain his footing. I didn't know about hyperthermia when I was a teenager. At any rate, it wouldn't have mattered. Harv's waders were full of water and it was time to go home. I never understood why he didn't want to go duck hunting again.

It didn't take long for Green Horn number two to enter the scene. His name was Billy Gay (not really). But he was a little on the sissy side from a sixteen-year-old perspective. Billy Gay always talked about the squirrel hunts he and his dad went on. I started to believe in him until he bragged about what a good shot he was and how his ten gauge could "reach up there and get 'em." That was my first clue something wasn't on the level.

My buddies and I were fairly good at squirrel hunting and we decided to see just how good this miniature Daniel Boone really was. One particular afternoon, the weather was windy with occasional showers. It was not the perfect day for hunting squirrels, but we were trying almost everything to get a shot. We managed to shake one out of its nest using a grape vine and my buddies quickly killed him. Billy Gay started whining about how he was "just about to pull the trigger." So we devised a plan. We would let Billy Gay shoot a few squirrel nests (which we usually didn't do). He had borrowed one of my guns. The first nest he shot at was missed completely. That was my second clue he was a Green Horn.

Finally, we found a large freshly made nest. There was a high possibility this event would be entertaining. Billy Gay shot the nest and the entire nest started shaking. He shot again and leaves started falling. After the third shot, a huge coon came crashing down to the ground. Billy Gay came running over to the dead coon and proudly proclaimed, "That's the biggest squirrel I've ever seen!" Yep, you guessed it—that was my third clue…Green Horn.

Challenge: Although these stories are true and meant to be entertaining, they show how easy it is to look down upon others who are not as proficient at outdoor recreation as others. Perhaps, instead of lording ourselves over people with less outdoor skill, we should learn to appreciate their strengths. Are there people in your extended family who care nothing for hunting? Do you treat them respect or disdain?

Thought: This story was not meant to trivialize the inherent danger in duck hunting nor the possibility of Billy Gay becoming my brother-in-law.

And just as you want people to treat you, treat them in the same way.
Luke 6:31

Seasons of Reflection

Hidden

My family and I lived in West Virginia for five years. One of my hunting buddies took me to his favorite "honey hole" located in the northwest region of the state. To say the area was mountainous would have been an understatement. This particular county was known for its large whitetail bucks and bear populations. It was early autumn and the leaves were a spectacular sight. Colors of every hue could be seen as the sun woke up the sleepy darkness.

I was hunting with a recurve and hoped to bag a decent deer on this early morning. However, the temperature was in the teens and about ten o'clock, I had to get down from my ladder stand and warm up. I was walking along the top of a ridge and noticed several scrapes as well as other deer signs. Since I had been hunting in my friend's stand, I didn't have my climb on stand. Therefore, I started looking for a natural place downwind of the major scrape to hide my scent as well as my silhouette.

About twenty yards from the scrape was the trunk of a very large tree. The tree must have fallen many years before for all of its limbs had long since rotted and disappeared. All that was left was the trunk, which was half rotted as well. In fact, there was enough room to lie down inside the tree since the top part of the butt had been eaten away by insects and decay. There was just enough room to wallow out a space large enough for my entire body. With a little rearranging of decaying bark, I was able to make a small shelf to rest my neck upon. I placed my bow across the top of the log perpendicular to the trunk. The only part of my body in plain view was my head, which was camouflaged by my toboggan and face paint. After relaxing for a few moments, the bright afternoon sun warmed things up and I dozed from noon to around three o'clock.

My deep sleep was interrupted by the sound of crunching leaves—a sound I had heard many times before. I knew exactly what to expect.

When I wormed my way into the log, it never dawned upon me I might see a bear. Flatlanders like me are not used to having such possibilities. I never imagined I might need to get out of the log in a hurry or climb a tree. If it was a bear, I prayed my face would be ugly enough to scare him away. At the very least, the bear was surely not acclimated to logs screaming threats in shear terror.

Suddenly the suspense and mind games were over, I looked slightly to my left and saw a fat six-point buck. He placed his nose directly into the scrape and without thinking I raised up from the log and in one fluid motion released my cedar shaft. I could see my shaft flying in slow motion toward the buck's vitals. I heard that familiar "thump" arrows make when they connect with their quarry. I had made a good hit and watched the buck closely as he bounced out of sight. I have lived that hunt a thousand times since it occurred. Without a doubt, it was one of my most memorable hunts. There is nothing like taking a buck with a bow from the ground, especially when the only blind used is natural cover.

Challenge: Many of us guys spend a lot of time hiding. We hide from ourselves, our wives, our friends, and most of all, from God. When is the last time you took a hard look at who you are? What is the total sum of your life? Do you like what you have become? What areas in your life need to change?

Thought: If you cannot live with yourself, how do you expect others to live with you?

> *But there is nothing covered up that will not be revealed, and hidden that will not be known, accordingly, whatever you have said in the dark shall be heard in the light, and what you have whispered in the inner rooms will be proclaimed upon the housetops.* Luke 12:2-3

> *Thou hast placed our iniquities before Thee, our secret sins in the light of Thy presence.* Psalm 90:8

Would not God find this out? For He knows the secrets of the heart.

Psalm 44:21

…the secrets of his heart are disclosed; and so he will fall on his face and worship God, declaring that God is certainly among you.

1 Corinthians 14:25

Awareness

Many years ago, a hunting buddy of mine, Kenny Williams, had a camp on a beautiful lake. We would stay in his cabin and hunt turkeys every spring. The house was located on a large bay that connected with the lake some mile or so from the cabin. The land across the bay was covered with hardwood ridges and turkeys were getting started very well but the land was closed to hunting. We kept up with one gobbler and eventually called him the Sultan because he seemed to be the dominant bird in the area. The Sultan roosted in virtually the same tree every year. We guessed his spurs to be around one and one half inches since we knew him to be five years old. Finally, the land where the Sultan was located was made available for hunting. Upon returning from another hunting location, Kenny heard the Sultan gobbling across the bay. He quickly placed his single barrel ten gauge into his canoe and headed for the other side of the bay. As he paddled across the bay, Kenny could hardly contain his excitement and thought to himself—"Today is the day I will kill this old tom. I'm sure he has the longest spurs of any turkey I have ever killed."

After dragging the canoe onto the bank, Kenny could hear the Sultan gobbling every breath. He quickly decided to find a place to sit, but could not find a suitable tree. There was no cover available except for a deep gully running from the top of the ridge to the waters edge. Suddenly, he remembered something Ben Lee had said on one of his instructional cassette tapes. Ben made the statement that he believed a wild turkey's senses were so acute that a man could crawl into a hole and call one time and the turkey would know exactly where he was. Kenny decided to try out Ben's theory. He hastily climbed down into the gulley and laid flat on his back. After running through a series of yelps and clucks, the Sultan fired back with great interest. Kenny stopped calling and waited. A few minutes later, he could hear the unmistakable sound of crunching leaves. His heart was racing as the gobbler drummed within a few yards of his location. The Sultan gobbled loudly and then walked directly to the gulley where Kenny was hiding. As the sound of crunching leaves grew louder, Kenny's heart raced faster and faster. He tried to guess the exact location the gobbler's head would appear and readied his shotgun.

Suddenly, the Sultan's head appeared. He was craning his neck looking directly into the gulley. Kenny was ready—laying flat on his back and gun pointed directly at the Sultan's head. As he pulled the trigger, the gun snapped without a roar. The Sultan was looking directly into the muzzle of a ten-gauge shotgun at virtually point blank range. At the snapping sound of the firing pin, the Sultan became aware of the situation. With eyes widened and yellow beak agape (Kenny swears to this day he heard the Sultan gasp for air), the Sultan made a leap into hyperspace that would make light speed seem like slow motion. In all the excitement, Kenny had forgotten to load his gun! He testified he had never seen a turkey with such a surprised look on his face. We never heard the Sultan gobble again. Kenny thinks he may have scared him to death.

Challenge: Are you aware of all the things trying to destroy your life? Sometimes, we let our guard down and walk directly into situations that are detrimental to our lives and relationships. What are the things threatening your well being right now? Is it a girlfriend or the temptation for an affair? Whatever they may be, don't walk blindly into them. Use your head. Use your faith. Use your legs—run! Stand on your commitment to do what is right.

Thoughts: Stay away from the dark gullies and pits of life—don't even look into them. As surely as you enter, there is an enemy waiting. Once you slide into them it is extremely difficult to get out. Only God and His mercy can lift you out again. Stay aware.

Can a man walk on hot coals and his feet not be scorched? So is the one who goes in to his neighbor's wife; whoever touches her will not go unpunished.   Proverbs 6:28-29

For the commandment is a lamp, and the teaching is light; and reproofs for discipline are the way of life, to keep you from the evil woman, from the smooth tongue of the adulteress. Do not desire her beauty in your heart, nor let her catch you with her eyes.

Proverbs 6:23-25

Now flee from youthful lusts...   *2 Timothy 2:22*

Safety First

Yeah, yeah, blah, blah, blah is the response of some outdoorsmen when it comes to safety. Safety should be our first consideration above all else. If someone is not hunting safely and will not receive correction, then don't hunt with them.

One beautiful fall afternoon, a friend of mine asked if I wanted to go rabbit hunting. He stated he had a few good beagles and a great place to hunt rabbits. This particular guy was a country boy and had hunted all of his life. I had never hunted with him but assumed he would know how to handle a firearm.

The ground was wet from a rainstorm the previous day. The air was cool and it was a great day to hunt rabbits. After bagging a few cottontails, the dogs struck another trail. My friend and I were standing in a road about sixty yards apart. The dogs circled and came directly between us. Suddenly, a rabbit appeared crossing the road between us. The rabbit was closer to him than me. As I watched my friend shoulder his shotgun, I could hardly believe he was going to shoot directly in my direction. I quickly fell to the ground as two shots roared. I could hear shot breaking through the tall weeds around me. As I returned to my feet, I quickly expressed my dissatisfaction with his choice of shots. He replied by stating, "I was shooting directly toward the ground." I replied, "Don't you know shot skips off the ground and even more so if it is wet? Furthermore, you shot directly toward *me!*"

My friend was now my ex-friend/hunting partner as he simply laughed it off. On this particular hunt, I was carrying some reloads. The crimped end of one shell had popped open leaving a hand full of shot in my pocket. I decided to play a joke on my unsuspecting ex-friend and quickly made my way to this guy to show him the seriousness of his offense. I started by asking if he could see any blood on my upper thigh while nervously pulling eight to ten shot out of my pocket. I continued by stating he had probably scarred my leg for life. His faced turned an ashen white as he began to apologize profusely. Then, he realized I was pulling a prank and started laughing again as I stated, "You really *could* have shot me, you know." He never took his offense seriously. But you can bank on one thing—I never went hunting with him again. Carelessness can kill you or someone you love.

Challenge: When you address your family members, do you do so with carelessness, harshness, or gentleness? If your wife or kids complain of your harshness, do you laugh it off? Careless speech is a serious offense to them and often ends in emotional separation. Your potential to permanently wound others needs to be taken seriously.

Thought: Verbally blasting others can leave scars for life… and that's no joke.

> *Let no unwholesome word proceed from your mouth, but only*
> *such a word as is good for edification according to the need of the*
> *moment, that it may give grace to those who hear.*   Ephesians 4:29

Ethics

I wish I could say I have behaved ethically in every hunting situation, but I cannot. Thank God by His grace we get more than one chance at this life. Bag limits, posted property, game laws, licenses, and the like are all very much a part of the hunting heritage. One great pioneer of hunting stated, "Ethics is when you do what is right when no one else is there to see you."

We have the *legal* right to hunt on the fence line of posted property in sight of hunters on the other side, but it isn't ethical to do so. We have the legal right to fish in the same spot as someone else. But if they arrived there first, it isn't ethical to do so. We have the legal right to hunt on the same ridge as another turkey hunter and call to the same bird, but is it ethical? We have the legal right to kill the bag limit each time we go hunting, but is it absolutely necessary to do so? We have the legal right to hunt waterfowl, but is it ethical to interrupt someone else's hunt by hunting too closely to their blind? We may have the legal right to ride your four-wheeler into the woods, but is it ethical to do so if you know others are hunting nearby?

On several occasions, I have threatened to give up hunting once and for all. Discourteous hunters, foul mouths, and trespassers have a way of dampening the spirit of the hunt. Times are changing. Hunting grounds that used to be available are being sold or posted. Housing developments and other construction plans are rapidly destroying prime wildlife habitats. Politicians threaten our very right to own firearms. Many American and global leaders as well as minority groups want to take away the enjoyment of our sport by making it illegal. They completely ignore the fact it was our money that renewed such vast populations of wildlife we now enjoy—not to mention the land in which they dwell.

No sir, it ain't like it used to be. I often wonder if this great sport will be able to withstand the constant barrage of negativity created by the media circus. Will my sons be able to pass this heritage to their kids? We cannot afford to be divided at this time in the history of our nation. Hunters are divided primarily because of our selfishness. It seems like killing an animal is more important to some than common courtesy. Hunters who trespass and poach game animals are not helping the overall image of hunters at all. Furthermore, there is nothing macho about killing over the legal bag limit. We need to respect posted property, private roads, and keep trash to ourselves. We need to treat others the way we want to be treated. I appreciate the work of many organizations that seek to restore wildlife habitat, hold hunter education classes, lobby Washington, and work tirelessly to preserve this great heritage of ours. Every hunter this day and time needs to support one of these organizations if indeed you care about the future of our sport.

Ethics has to start somewhere. We need to treat others with the respect that is due. Before carrying out an action that is unethical, stop and consider what you are doing. Consider the long-term effects of your decision. When making decisions that will affect other hunters or sportsmen, ask yourself, "How would I feel if someone were doing this to me?" Again, we need to do what is right, even if no one else is looking. Let's work together to ensure our outdoor heritage continues.

Challenge: Are you more concerned with bagging a trophy than preserving our sport? Some will go to any lengths to kill an animal and their antics are slowly ruining it for all of us. Name three areas in which you can improve when it comes to ethics. Make a decision to change these areas today.

Thought: Would God be pleased with the way I have treated my fellow sportsman?

> *Therefore, however you want people to treat you, so treat them, for this is the Law and the Prophets.*   *Matthew 7:12*

Rite of Passage

My very first squirrel hunt will never be forgotten. I was seven years old when my dad promised to take me squirrel hunting. Santa Claus brought my very first game vest just like dad's as well as a pair of green rubber boots. A trip to the local sporting goods store topped off my hunting clothing with a nice brown hat. I don't know what those hats were called—sort of shaped like a fisherman's hat on a box of frozen fish sticks. I can hardly believe some people still wear these odd looking "lids" as it were.

Dad woke me up early in the morning by whispering into my ear—"Let's go kill some fuzzy tails." He always got up a little early to fix pancakes or biscuits before the hunt. Dad was never one to head to the woods on an empty stomach. We quickly got dressed and ate breakfast. I still remember the smell of his coffee as he slurped down a cup. Then, we always whispered back and forth so we wouldn't wake up the rest of the family. Finally, Dad would lace up his hunting boots and off we would go—so the routine continued until my teenage years.

I remember sitting beside a large red oak and looking intently into the trees. The smell of the woods made a distinct impression on me. I never forgot it. To this day, every time I enter the woods and smell that familiar odor my mind drifts back to that fall morning so many years ago. High in the fork of a red oak tree I noticed a brown ball of fur. I could hear the squirrel cutting acorns and dropping pieces of hull directly in front of us. I slowly raised the borrowed twenty gauge and pulled the trigger. Down came my first squirrel with a thud. "I got him!" I exclaimed. "Yes, you did, son. Way to go!" responded Dad. "You are now a bona fide squirrel hunter," he added. From that point on, I was hooked. The smell of gunpowder from the ejected shell marked my senses as well. I still love the smell of gunpowder after a shell has been shot. In fact, it has become a kind of ritual for me and my children. Each time one of my kids killed their first squirrel, I held the empty shell up to their nose for a good sniff. Then I would remind them never to forget that smell—the smell that marks a hunter.

In American culture there are no rites of passage for young men. For instance, exactly *when* did you become a man? Did you become a man at the age of thirteen…fourteen… eighteen…twenty-one? Did you become a man when you landed your first job or after you were married? Many of us have always longed for a particular event to establish our manhood. Truth is, many of us do not know how to answer this question. Perhaps, you are reading this and you are not a man at all—you are a woman. *When* did you become a woman?

Rites of passage—they *are* important. Almost all cultures have some type of rite of passage for young people. Those of us who love the outdoors have a great opportunity to create rites of passage for our young outdoorsmen. When I was a youngster, it was a tradition to smear blood across the face of the young hunter when he killed his first buck. Although some may not like such a tradition, it made a statement to the young hunter—"Today you have become a deer hunter!"

Challenge: Create some rites of passage for your young sons and grandsons so they will know they have become a man—a man who unashamedly hunts.

Thought: There is only one rite of passage that *really* matters—that moment we are initiated into the family of God.

> *When I was a child, I used to speak as a child, think as a child, reason as a child; when I became a man, I did away with childish things.*   *1 Corinthians 13:11*

If you would like to know how to become a follower of Christ, please consult the back of the book, beginning on page 157.

Merrily Muddy

Mud and duck hunting go hand in hand. Last year my nine-year-old son, Reed, and I met our good friend, Jerry Gaddy, in the Mississippi Delta. Duck hunting is always unpredictable but we could hardly wait on sunrise the first morning of the hunt. After scarfing down breakfast, we loaded our gear in the back of the Polaris and headed for the blind. Delta gumbo mud sticks like none other. As we made our way to the blind, mud flew up and out from under the grinding machine. After driving through eighteen inches of water for several hundred yards, we arrived at the pit blind. The sounds of waterfowl on the roost were abundant. We hurriedly unpacked our gear, placed our decoys and settled into the blind. As we waited upon the highly anticipated legal shooting moment, my son was extremely excited about the morning's hunt. As light began to illuminate the star filled sky, whistling wings could be heard overhead. There's something about that sound that makes a water fowler's heart pump a little faster. Mallards, Pintails, Gadwals, Teal, and Shovelers made up most of the activity. Geese were also abundant, but were not the targeted bird for the day.

Wave after wave of ducks flew over our blind. Enough worked the decoys to provide some exciting recreation. After the legal limit was taken, we reminisced about the hunt. The last few birds were quite an experience to remember. Jerry was shooting at a green-winged teal and squeezed off a single shot as the group rapidly buzzed the decoys. We sat in amazement as three teal fell from the sky! Jerry said, "Tim, did you shoot at the teal in front of the blind?" "No, I replied, I was shooting at the birds on the other side of the blind!" "Can you believe that," he replied, "I just killed three in one shot!" Sure enough, there were three birds floating on the water.

As we picked up the decoys, my son, Reed, fell backwards into the shallow water and mud. It did not bother him at all. He loves the mud! Why do we love mud when we are little boys or for that matter when we grow up? The loaded Polaris slipped and spun all the way back to the camp house. You could smell the mud baking on the engine and exhaust pipe. You know that smell don't you?

After cleaning the birds, we hopped on our four-wheeler and hit the mud again. I have heard of people actually tearing the fenders off their four wheelers as delta gumbo mud caked so badly around the wheels they would no longer turn. The trick is to find water—when tires begin to gum up with mud, quickly run into the water. The water loosens the mud and frees the wheels to continue pulling. Slinging mud and water is the stuff good duck hunts (or bad ones) are made of. I love it!

Challenge: Is there a nagging persistent issue that is stuck to you like mud? Something you can't seem to shake off? Something tearing the fenders off your marriage? Time to hit the water!

Thought: The life giving flow of God's grace will set you free from all that bogs you down.

> But the wicked are like the tossing sea, for it cannot be quiet, and its waters toss up refuse and mud. "There is no peace," says my God, "for the wicked."   Isaiah 57:20-21

> He who believes in Me, as the Scripture said, "From his innermost being will flow rivers of living water."   John 7:38

Mobility, Part 1

Movement is such a God-given thing. You don't realize how much it means until you loose it. It is one of the greatest trump cards in the hunter's hand. The following three devotions will address this topic. Without a doubt, changing locations while hunting turkey is one of the most strategic things we are required to do. Of course, movement is necessitated when hunting small game and upland birds. One can also utilize this important tool while stand hunting for deer with the exception of climbing stands. If the hunter is hunting from a ground blind, ladder stand, or lock-on, he can strategically move when the moment calls for it. However, it must be stated, knowing the terrain is imperative before using this strategy.

Two of my best bucks to date, have been killed due to a strategically designed encounter. One evening, I was hunting from a ladder stand when a nice tall eight pointer and three does made their way down an adjacent ridge. This was one of those dry, quite afternoons. Squirrels had been scurrying about all afternoon. You could literally hear them throughout the woods as they chased one another from tree to tree. I knew it would be impossible to sneak up on all four deer with such dry conditions. Additionally, shooting would be impossible beyond fifty yards or so due to the thickness of the surrounding cover.

Suddenly, it dawned upon me all I needed to do was *sound* like a squirrel. I waited until the deer traveled out of sight. They were now traveling between the ridge upon which they had entered the woods and the one on which I hunted. If I could get ahead of them while they were crossing the valley between the two ridges, I would be in great position for an ambush. The wind was right—I was downwind and they could not see my movement while down in the valley. Therefore, I reasoned, all I had to do was fool their ears.

After quietly unloading my rifle and lowering it carefully to the ground, I quickly but silently climbed down from the ladder stand. Then, I rhythmically skipped very rapidly across the leaves making a lot of noise. After five or six skips, I stood for a moment and shuffled one of my feet. Interestingly enough, I sounded exactly like a squirrel. I knew I must cover a lot of ground very rapidly to pull this thing off. I quickly covered one hundred and fifty yards or so until I knew I must be close to the area the deer would surely travel over the top of the ridge. If all went according to plan, the deer would reveal themselves within shooting range of my position.

After traveling as far as I dared, I quickly sat down and rested the rifle on my left knee. Less than a minute later, I heard the sound of crunching leaves just below the edge of the ridge. The deer were traveling directly in front of me but still out of sight. A doe appeared first at twenty yards and immediately noticed me. However, she had not begun to act nervously…yet. I was looking at her directly through my scope doing my best to evaporate into the ground cover. Suddenly, she started the stomping game and I knew I had been busted. However, I could still hear approaching steps and noticed a deer moving slowly to her right. The first thing I saw in my scope was the tip of antlers. Slowly, I moved the reticle of my scope to the head of the oncoming buck. He stopped. All that was showing was his eyes and rack. The doe was stomping more emphatically by this time. Time was ticking and I knew this game was soon to be over. I expected the deer to bolt down into the valley any second, which would cancel my opportunity for a descent shot. The buck took two more cautious steps toward my location therefore exposing his neck. Mistake— one shot later, the buck was lying on the ground. To this date, he is still the best eight pointer I have taken.

Okay, the results could have been different. But this day, the scales had tipped in my favor. Without a doubt, this buck would not be hanging on my wall if I had not taken a chance. It was better than sitting in my stand wishing I had placed the stand on the adjacent ridge.

Mobility, Part 2

Last year, my two sons and I were hunting a farm in Kentucky. This particular farm had two main stands. Each stand was located on the opposite end of the farm approximately four hundred yards apart. We had been communicating with one another using hand held radios. These small hand held units are great when hunting with teenagers or buddies you want to stay in contact with during the hunt.

My oldest son contacted me concerning a buck he was observing located between my stand and theirs. He stated the buck's rack to be "way outside his ears." Of course, this interested me. Upon further enquiry, the radios went dead. I knew the batteries were weak, but to go out at this particular moment was a bummer indeed. I needed a little more information.

The buck was about three hundred yards from my sons but much closer to me. However, I could not see the deer. He had traveled through a grown up field while chasing a few does and had recently jumped a fence leading him into a section of woods within my field of view. Although he was in front of me, he could easily skirt my position by traveling on the lower side of the sloping woodlot. It suddenly occurred to me to try my cell phone. Just maybe, I could talk with my son, one more time. Surprisingly, the phone connection was strong enough to converse with my son one more time. I found out which side of the woodlot he had entered and surmised he was probably traveling the lower side of the woodlot as I had anticipated.

It was time to make a decision. Should I sit it out or take a chance trying to intercept the buck? I elected to slowly make my way toward the buck. My stand overlooked a field that bordered the small woodlot the deer had entered. Upon slowly entering the woodlot, a doe bolted away in the opposite direction. Suddenly, another doe almost ran over me while a small buck chased her in my direction. Moments later, the deer raced off in another direction.

I knew the big buck must be very close if he were still in the small wood-lot. Suddenly, a doe came running toward me from the direction in which I had anticipated the big buck traveling. She was running as if something were chasing her. Part of me wanted to believe it would be the big buck but I *really* expected it to be the small buck I had just observed.

Suddenly, I heard the familiar sound of crunching leaves and grunting. I strained to see through the honeysuckle thicket when white antlers appeared before me...*wide*, white antlers. My heart began to beat in wild expectation. I could not believe this great deer was so very close to me and had not discovered my presence. The thicket provided such adequate cover the buck almost eluded me.

After calling my sons and asking them to join me, we celebrated while holding a twenty-two inch wide rack with large bases and ten points. He was a dandy indeed. This beautiful buck was my best deer to date. Once again, had I not moved, this buck would have probably been killed by a neighboring landowner.

Mobility, Part 3

A few years ago, I was watching a big gobbler feeding in a shelled corn-field. I could tell by looking at him through my binoculars he was a mature bird. He was approximately one hundred and seventy-five yards away. The field was wide open and the gobbler would not respond to calling. I was trying to figure out a way to get ahead of him but I was backed against a river and there was no way to move without giving away my position. As I sat debating what to do, I noticed a small briar thicket about ten yards in circumference. I suppose it was a sinkhole the farmer had planted around. At any rate, that ole gobbler looked as if he was going to pass directly behind the thicket if he stayed on his current course. I devised a plan.

Now understand I love to call turkeys and watch them strut and gobble, but I am not opposed to bushwhacking one every now and then. Besides, it has been my experience that sneaking up on ole tom will test every ounce of woodsmanship and skill you possess. I am convinced that some turkeys have become call shy to the extent the only practical way to kill them is to bushwhack 'em.

I am *not* advocating waiting on a gobbler to cross a particular field at a certain time or place because the local land owner has seen him do this repeatedly. The hunter sits, waits, and shoots. Neither am I advocating sitting over bait, which is illegal in every state in which I hunt. These tactics are not the same thing to that which I am referring. If the method you employ is legal, you then have to decide if it is ethical. Some feel bushwhacking a turkey is not an ethical means of pursuing this noble bird. However, it has never bothered *me* to bushwhack ole tom and many times has made a very exciting hunt—to each his own.

I decided to watch through my binoculars and after that ole tom was completely behind the briar thicket, I would make my move. The thicket appeared to be thick enough to hide my movements. When it comes to bushwhacking turkeys—it is all or nothing. Either I beat him or he beats me. I am completely satisfied with the many times the turkey has beaten me. I know the odds are against me before I even try. Besides, it just leaves the door open for another contest on another day. My motto is— "kill him or scare him." It was time to make my move.

As soon as the turkey was thoroughly out of sight, I ran as quickly as possible across the wide-open field. The field was damp due to a light rain the night before which helped muffle my steps. However, I tried to run as quietly as possible. While crossing the field, I was making a mental note as to where I thought the turkey might be in relation to my angle and the thicket. He was moving at a fairly good pace and I needed to keep this in mind so the bird would not emerge from behind the thicket before I was in shooting range. Upon reaching the thicket, I readied my gun and ever so slowly peaked around the thicket. I could see through the edge of the tangled briars a big black form coming into view. I had been standing there all of one minute. As the gobbler picked blades of grass, I carefully raised my gun. Slowly, he fed beyond the thicket and I killed him at thirty yards. He never knew I was there. This was a three-year-old bird with nice spurs.

Once again, sometimes your hunting situation necessitates movement. You must maintain a mental state of mobility while turkey hunting as well as deer hunting. It needs to be said that movement will many times spoil the hunt. But this suspense is what makes the stalk exciting. A series of moves and counter moves livens up the hunt. Don't be afraid to move. Use every available strategy to tip the odds in your favor. Besides, it's a lot of fun and can make the hunt much more interesting.

Challenge: Sometimes in life you've just got to move. Aggressive decision-making can be a virtue but can also be risky. Those who utilize the stock market know how vital it is to make good solid decisions quickly. On the other hand, there are also decisions that require a lot of forethought before making the call. In making life's major decisions, what if you had someone to coach you when and when not to move? What if someone who had made the journey before and could see the future offered all the counsel you needed? Life would certainly have fewer regrets and the emotional scars that go along with them—*and you could make your moves with confidence in the outcome.*

Thoughts: One of the reasons God gives His Holy Spirit to those who ask is to help people make good, solid decisions. His specialty is counseling people as they navigate throughout life. Do you *know* Him? Don't you *need* Him? I sure do.

> *Thou dost know when I sit down and when I rise up; Thou dost understand my thought from afar.* Psalm 139:2

> *I have restrained my feet from every evil way, that I may keep Thou word.* Psalm 119:101

> *Let me hear Thou lovingkindness in the morning; for I trust in Thee; Teach the way in which I should walk; For to Thee I lift up my soul.* Psalm 143:8

> *Every man's heart is right in his own eyes, But the Lord weighs the hearts.* Proverbs 21:2

> *...for in Him we live and move and exist...* Acts 17:28

> *And your ears will hear a word behind you, "This is the way, walk in it," whenever you turn to the right or to the left.* Isaiah 30:21

Memories

My late friend, Billy Hillman, was a true sportsman. He taught me how to bow hunt and many other things about the great outdoors. We hunted deer, rabbit, duck, dove, turkey, and fished together. I was with Billy when I heard my first turkey gobble and He taught me the difference between a hen and gobbler track. As a young teenager, Billy was my senior by ten years. He was a forester and would sometimes take me with him while cruising timber. I idolized him during those youthful years and wanted to be just like him when I grew up. Sadly, I didn't realize at the time Billy had a lot of adult-sized problems with which he was struggling. When I was twenty-nine years old, Billy took his own life. One of the hardest things I have ever done was speak at Billy's funeral. Today, I still have my first compass that he gave me. That compass has helped me find my way home many times and I don't want to take a chance of losing it. Today, it rests on a shelf in my turkey beard case.

Every fall while sitting on my deer stand, and every spring that rolls around, I think of Billy and his contribution to my life. I sure do miss him. I'm sure you are thinking of someone right now that you miss each hunting season. I still remember the hunts Billy and I had together in the snow and rain. One time while hunting in the swamp, we were driving down a muddy road covered with ten inches of water. It was steadily raining. I loved that old 1977 Bronco he used to drive. It would go through anything. On this particular drive, things were going very smoothly when all of a sudden the entire truck bucked up and down. We both hit our heads on the ceiling of the cab. Billy had run over a small stump that was covered with water. We laughed together as we discovered what had created this monstrous jolt to his Bronco.

Then there was the time we picked up the deer dogs and put them into the back seat. One of them, a big redbone hound, had gas extremely bad. That dog pert near ran us out of the truck! We tried to laugh but were choking too much to do so. Billy had to pull the Bronco over since his eyes had watered so he could no longer see the road.

I'll never forget watching him shoot that big doe with his bow or the day I missed the eight pointer, or that boat load of bream we caught, or…or… I sure do miss him. Through the years, I have come to realize that building intentional memories is the most lasting gift we give to those whom we love. Therefore, I have made it my ambition to intentionally plan things that will build positive memories into the lives of my children. Yes, bad things happen also, but it seems the good always overshadows the bad when we scroll through our memory files.

Challenge: According to the way you are living right now, when you are gone, will memories of you bring a smile to the face of others or feelings of regret?

Thought: Memories *of* us will outlive the times *with* us. Let's make them count.

…you always think kindly of us…   *1 Thessalonians 3:6*

Illusion

Things are not always as they seem to be. Several years ago, I was hunting at Land Between the Lakes in Kentucky. Many roads were closed to walk-in traffic only. Through the years, I had selected one of these roads as my favorite hunting spot. The opening day of the season, I discovered someone had beaten me to the draw and parked at my intended walk-in hunting location. I knew the road was several miles long and decided to walk the road and maybe catch up to the hunter in front of me. It was still pitch black and I had a good thirty-minute walk to get to the place I wanted to hunt. I had already decided if I caught up to the person in front of me to give him the first right of refusal if a turkey gobbled.

About half a mile into my brisk morning walk, I heard someone imitating the sound of a barred owl. The hunter was no more than two hundred yards from my position. I decided to pick up the pace in hopes of catching him before he set out after a turkey. That way, if I heard a gobbler, I could be sure the other hunter had not already started toward him. After covering about one hundred and fifty yards, I saw them. Yep, you read it right, "them." I had not anticipated there being more than one hunter. Now the situation would be even more difficult. But hey, there was plenty of room for all of us, so no need to get upset, right?

As I walked toward the two or three hunters, I politely said, "Good morning to ya." None of the now apparent *three* hunters spoke a word. I must have really made these guys mad; the least they could do is speak. I mean it's not like I'm going to run ahead of them and scare the turkey off the roost. Besides, this is public hunting and I have just as much right to be in the area as they do! So there!

As I continued getting closer to the three hunters, it became increasingly apparent why they had not responded to my greeting. In the predawn darkness, I had just spoken to an uprooted tree. Nope, things are not always as they seem. I could have sworn that the uprooted tree was three hunters silhouetted against the dawn-lit sky. But I was wrong. Have you ever been dead wrong about something?

Challenge: Sometimes our perception of how things are is very convoluted. We really believe our understanding is absolutely correct but nothing can be further from the truth. There is always the possibility we are wrong. How do *you* discern truth?

Thoughts: Have you ever marred someone's reputation by spreading *your* perception of a given situation? How do you *know* you were correct? When we lose our plumb line for discerning right and wrong, each man does what is right in his own eyes. The Word of God, the Bible, is our plumb line for truth.

> *Let no unwholesome word proceed out of your mouth, but only such a word as good for edification according to the need of the moment, so that it will give grace to those who hear.*   Ephesians 4:29

Curiosity

One spring season I was turkey hunting on Fort Campbell Military Installation. I could not believe the number of turkeys in this particular area. While I had heard fifty Rio Grande turkeys gobbling at one time, I had never heard that many Eastern birds gobbling in the same area. An added bonus to the numerous turkeys was getting to see all the big deer sign. Fort Campbell has produced some monster bucks through the years. Surprisingly, I do not hunt there often because it's such a hassle getting your permit and those serving in the military always get first choice of the areas.

On this beautiful sun-filled morning, I was moving from one side of the hunting area to the other, when I noticed a young fox squirrel hurriedly climbing a tree. I suppose he was eating something on the ground in the edge of a field when I startled him. It was mid-day as often is when one sees a fox squirrel. I was fully camouflaged with head net and gloves on my hands. I decided to play with the young squirrel for a few minutes. I casually walked over to the twenty-foot tree he had selected as a security post.

Slowly, I lifted my arm and began to twitch my forefinger while making a loud smooching noise. I wasn't sure how he was going to react but slowly he started descending the tree absolutely fixated on my finger. Every time he would twitch his tail, I would wiggle my finger. He kept getting closer and closer until he was about seven or eight inches away from my hand (kinda like the kid who cast his bass plug at the cottonmouth swimming across the pond—once he snagged him, he didn't know what to do with him). I wasn't sure what I was going to do if all of a sudden he decided to pounce on said squealing finger. Was he mad, curious, or in love? Whatever his motivation, he seemed to be completely mesmerized.

Although his movements were unpredictable, I couldn't help but wonder what was going on in that little brain of his. I wasn't sure what he was going to do, but when he got about three inches away, it was time to end the game. I jerked my hand away and hollered right into his little fury face. With eyes bulging, he feverishly spun around kicking bark into my face and headed toward the sun. Up, up, up, he rocketed until there was no more tree left to climb. There he sat peering down at me as if to say, what in the rotten nut is that?

I could literally see his sides pumping breathlessly. My heart was pumping nervously as well. We saluted each other as fitting for all military personnel and went our separate ways. I learned several valuable lessons from my observation of that young fox squirrel.

Challenge: Are you fooled by Satan's clever disguises? How does he camouflage himself when attempting to deceive you? Your curiosity to answer the seductive call of lust will lead to your undoing.

Thoughts: Satan makes you think his attempts at destroying you are mere games. What types of sights and sounds does he use to mesmerize you? Remember, run toward the Son.

…Satan disguises himself as an angel of light.

2 Corinthians 11:14

Predictability

Animals of all kinds are predictable and hunters take advantage of these patterns every time an animal is killed or caught in a trap. I will never forget the first mink I caught in a trail set. I could tell by his tracks that he was hopping over a small log repeatedly. With a devilish grin I placed a number one leg hold trap precisely where the minks tracks betrayed his habitual actions. I knew he would hop that ole log and land directly in my trap. That is exactly what happened. There was only one problem. The night I set the trap, thunderstorms brought about an inch of rain and consequently, the small branch upon which I had set the trap was swollen with water.

The next morning, I discovered both my trap and the drag were not only under water, but swept away by the current. I waded with my hip boots as deep as possible and placed a long stick in the water blindly trying to fish out the trap. Each time I ran the long stick into the water, I had hopes of hanging the wire to which my trap was tied. About the fifth or sixth attempt, I felt a tension on the stick and pulled the trap wire out of the water enough to get my hands on it. As I slowly pulled the trap chain, I could feel a tension on the trap. Needless to say, I was exhilarated when I saw a buck mink drowned in my trap. He was an older mink with thick fur and brought a good price from the fur buyer.

Then there was the time I kept seeing three coyotes running together on our farm. Each time, they would head toward a particular corner of our farm and go out of sight over a certain hill. I knew they had to be exiting the property in the northeast corner of the field. My son, Reed, and I happened to be setting traps on this particular afternoon and were returning to the truck around sunset. We noticed the three coyotes frolicking in the horse pasture and they noticed us as well. Predictably, they headed toward the very corner of the property where three traps awaited them. Our spirits were high the next morning, as we knew the odds were good we would have at least one of the coyotes. As our truck topped the ridge, we noticed two of the coyotes were snared and one had been caught in a leg hold trap. We discovered one to be a big male and the other two were females. Reed and I caught five coyotes in two days around that same location. Their predictable pattern had been their demise.

What about you? We know God clearly warns us that His enemy and ours is out to trap us. Satan wants to make us look like a fool and utterly destroy all that is meaningful to us. He preys on our predictability. Maybe it is our greed, pride, or lust that leads us into predictable patterns. Satan is not all knowing like God but he knows how to observe our movements and set traps for us at the most opportune times.

Take lust for instance. If you are being tempted to look at pornography through a particular website or bookstore, don't go there. If you regularly fall to this type of ensnarement, it will not stay a secret forever. Satan is tracking your habitual behavior and will make sure you are exposed. Incidentally, when you find yourself falling repeatedly, how do you live with *yourself*? If a man can't live with himself, he is in bad shape. Besides, God observes *all* we do and looks upon our heart and motivation. You are only fooling yourself. Therefore, it is not how well we hide from our wife that matters but how honest we are with ourselves and God. Sometimes, we need to ask a trusted friend for help or come completely clean and confess to our spouse this particular sin.

Maybe your temptation is *real* flesh—a girl in high school or woman at work or even church. Each time you near her, lust comes alive in your soul and you actually look forward to the engagements where you know she will be present. Your mind often wanders—"Does she think I am good looking or well built?" The mind game continues until one day she drops a small hint that she is thinking of you also. What do you do? You better run and run hard! What you fail to consider is Satan has been working both sides of this equation and plans to destroy you both. The girl in high school who has already revealed she is ready to go farther than you have gone before—flee her like the plague. Likewise, a woman who is betraying her husband will betray you as well. Her snare may look good and smell sweet but the end of her noose around your neck is certain death. The harder you struggle to free yourself, the more deadly her grip becomes.

There are certain places we must avoid if we are to keep our lives from becoming a statistic. Just as the mink or coyote can be easily trapped if observed long enough, our enemy will pattern you if you frequently flirt with sexual temptations. One day, he will have the perfect gal waiting for you. He has been grooming her for a long time to specifically destroy you. She may or may not be aware of his deception. Either way, the man of God must not be fooled by these traps. God did not create you for hand-to-hand combat with sexual temptation—run with all your might into the sanctuary of the Lord where He can change your heart and perspective on this powerful temptation. If you fight on your own, you will surely fail.

I love to trap foxes. But the fox that has been caught before and managed to escape is extremely difficult to fool again. Sadly, men are not that way. We can potentially fall to sexual temptation repeatedly. One man of God stated it this way; "God is most unreal to us when sexual temptation takes over." For this reason, we must renew our minds daily and surrender our wills to God. We live in a culture that constantly slams us with sexual images and titillations of every kind. There is no way to stay free of these body grippers unless we walk closely with the Lord Jesus. He alone can restore us and keep us free.

Challenge: *Whatever* it takes both practically and spiritually to stay free of sexual immorality, this is what you must do. Deal ruthlessly with this sin. It does not make a good bed partner. Remember, you are not alone in dealing with this temptation for *every man* must fight this fight.

Thought: If you continue making tracks on the lustful path you are on, how long do you think it will take Satan to outsmart you? One preacher stated it very clearly:

Sin will keep you longer than you wanted to stay.
Sin will cost you more than you wanted to pay.

Now flee youthful lusts, and pursue righteousness, faith, love and peace, with those who call on the Lord from a pure heart.

2 Timothy 2:22

Unimaginable

Ice is cold but can be hot enough to burn you. Ice is wet but can also be very dry. Ice is usually white but can sometimes be black. Ice can be thick but just as often thin. Ice is unpredictable. Ice can be smooth or rough—slippery or provide traction. It can be so much fun and yet so deadly. Nature is filled with uncertainties and dangers. Yet, there are some things we can do to lessen our chances of becoming a statistic.

When I was fourteen years old, my friend and I decided to go squirrel hunting. My dad acted as the chauffeur and dropped us off near our hunting spot at 6:30 a.m. We had to walk across a cow pasture to get to the area that promised to produce the quarry we pursued. Half way across the pasture was a small branch. On this particular morning, the branch was frozen since the temperature had been in the teens for the previous few days. The grass in the pasture was also frozen as evidenced by the crunching beneath my feet.

I have always been able to jump fairly well and was selected as one of the long jumpers and triple jumpers on my high school track team. Jumping ditches, creeks, and the like has been a lot of fun for me during my days afield. However, this particular branch was beyond my ability to traverse. Therefore, we looked for a suitable bridge provided by nature to get to the other side. We discovered a small tree that had fallen across the branch and elected to use it as a footbridge. I decided to go first and made it just fine until I had trouble climbing the opposite bank of the branch. I needed a little more help and elected to grab an old root sticking out from the bank. As I pulled on the root and started climbing the slippery bank in front of me, the root suddenly snapped and my forward momentum quickly reversed itself. I found myself falling backwards in slow motion. Funny how the mind does this when you are headed toward a catastrophe.

Instantaneously, I felt the frigid water engulf my entire body. I can truly say this is the only time I can remember ever floating my hat on an icy creek. I was totally submerged for what seemed like eternity. Upon surfacing, I gasped for air as if it were my last breath. Frantically, I scrambled up the bank I was initially trying to reach. Slowly, my second lesson came into focus—when falling into subzero water, always climb out the same direction you entered or otherwise you are soaking wet and *still* on the wrong side of the creek!

To make matters worse, my friend was not very sympathetic. In fact, he didn't even laugh. He was upset our hunt was ruined because I wasn't "tough enough to stick it out." I decided to show him just how tough I really was. We walked for another quarter of a mile until we got to the woods. I sat beside a big pine tree for about half an hour until I could no longer feel my fingers. Tough or not, I had to get home. When you get cold enough, it doesn't matter what friends think any longer. Pride takes a backseat to common sense.

My friend and I made it back to the main highway about forty-five minutes later. By this time, I was *really* cold and hyperthermia was setting in. At the time, I didn't even know such a thing existed. I asked my friend to go into a store, call my dad, and ask him to pick us up. He did so, but did not tell my dad I was soaking wet and standing outside in eighteen-degree weather. Consequently, my dad was in no hurry to pick us up and we waited for another hour or more before he finally arrived. Common sense is what saved my life that day. One of the storeowners was burning trash in a barrel and I stood beside the fire for an hour trying to keep warm until my dad arrived.

When I finally reached home, I took off my wet clothing and got into the bed piled high with covers. It was a good thirty minutes before I stopped shivering and the feeling started to slowly creep back into my extremities.

You may be thinking of a moment when you also experienced the chill of icy cold water. People lose their lives almost every year while fishing or duck hunting in frigid temperatures. It is important that all of us take the necessary precautions to ensure this doesn't happen. The time to prepare is *before* the mishap. When hunting in wet and cold conditions, always have a way to build a fire quickly. There are many packets containing the appropriate supplies on the market today. At the very least, one needs a waterproof container with matches and tinder/kindling inside that can be used to start a fire. It is also a good idea to carry extra clothing in a water-tight plastic bag when hunting from a boat. These preparations can save your life when the unthinkable happens.

It is our nature to think, "It will never happen to me." That's what my friend thought when he was climbing his deer stand with a loaded gun and the gun discharged beside his head. That's what another friend thought when he hung helplessly upside down from his tree stand until he cut himself loose. He managed to escape with a few broken ribs. A relative of mine had his big toe shot off by his brother as they were crossing a fence. Another friend is permanently disabled due to a fall from his deer stand and still another was completely paralyzed due to a fall from a ladder stand. *All* of these guys were seasoned hunters. They just got careless.

Many of us would never think of sitting in a tree stand without a safety harness or ride in a car without seatbelts. Why? These safety devices save lives—that's why. Then why don't we pay equal attention for our safety after we die? Make no mistake about it—hell is not a fun place. And incidentally, hell was not created for man anyhow, but for the devil and all of his demons. Yet, all of those who do not have a relationship with Christ will spend eternity there separated from God. Don't think, "This will never happen to me." As God lives, yes it will unless you take the necessary precautions.

It needs to be said here the best thing about becoming a follower of Christ is not missing hell but having His presence in your life *now*. Going to heaven is an excellent benefit to this relationship but is not the reason we want to "get saved." That word "saved" means not only saved *from* hell but *unto* a life given to God. It's not about giving up stuff or becoming good enough to get to heaven. You cannot do it! Only Christ was good enough to pay the penalty for your sin. Only through Christ can we get to heaven as well as experience His awesome presence *now*— when we need it!

Some of you reading this have loved ones who have been praying for you for years—that you would come to know the God they love. Don't you understand? God has not come to take away from you, but to give life to you. He wants to teach you how to *live* instead of merely *exist*. This relationship with God is what makes the outdoor experience rich indeed.

Our pride is what keeps us away from God. It has been that way since sin entered the human race. Yes, I suppose you are just as good as those professing Christians, but all of us will fall without God's strength. Besides, you are not responsible for those who do not wear a safety harness but you are responsible for you.

Accordingly, you wouldn't say, "We'll he's not a *hunter* because he hunts unethically or dangerously." And you probably wouldn't say, "Because *some* hunters are not ethical, then *all* hunters are unethical." A person like this may not be representative of a good hunter, but he is *still* a hunter nonetheless. This is the same treatment the anti-hunting establishment gives us and it's not fair is it? If you impose this same principle upon the Christian community saying *all* Christians are hypocrites, then you have judged us unfairly. Just because *some* may be hypocrites doesn't mean we *all* are.

Even so, don't look to those who are not living as Christians ought to live as an excuse to live the way you want to live. Look to Christians who *are* living as Christ would have them. I've never met a person who regretted getting their life right with God. However, I have heard an innumerable number state they "wished they had not waited so long to do so."

Challenge: We fall so we can learn to pick ourselves up, but when we fall from grace, there is no second chance. Have the practical lessons in life taught you anything about eternal truths? Today is the day for your life to change forever. Secure yourself to Jesus.

Thoughts: To have a counterfeit, you must first have that which is authentic. Hypocrites are substitutes for the real thing. It would be unthinkable to stop hunting because of a few outlaws. In the same way, it is unimaginable to think one would prepare for earthly dangers and completely avoid preparing for eternity because of a few counterfeits.

> *He who trusts in his riches will fall but the righteous will flourish like the green leaf.* Proverbs 11:28

> *Therefore let him who thinks he stands take heed lest he fall.* 1 Corinthians 10:12

> *…you have fallen from grace.* Galatians 5:4

> *Now to Him who is able to keep you from stumbling, and to make you stand in the presence of His glory blameless with great joy, to the only God our Savior, through Jesus Christ our Lord, be glory, majesty, dominion, and authority, before all time and now and forever. Amen.* Jude 1:24-25

The Great Bush Debate

Every few years, there seems to be a new camouflage on the market designed to fool even the most sharp-eyed quarry. Goullie suits came out via the military and have proven to be an effective means of camouflaging oneself from the enemy. However, for the purpose of hunting big game, I just can' bring myself to wear one. I think it is because I am not sure there is no such thing as Bigfoot and many other hunters out there secretly feel the same way. Therefore, to walk around the woods hunkered over in a Bigfoot suit is invitation for fire to say the least. I can just see some guy imagining his name in the newspaper having bagged the first baby Bigfoot. Simply stated, I just don't want to be anyone's trophy.

Things change. Leafy patterns are all the rage these days. I'm referring to those garments that have leaves sewn into the fabric. They stick out from one's torso and really do give a 3-D effect. Although I like the way they look on the clothing, I just can't bring myself to wear a hat with fake leaves sewn onto it. At any rate, I did purchase a hunting vest from Whitewater that has these type leaves sewn onto the garment and absolutely love it. The vest's long sleeves (covered with leaves) offer a reasonable degree of warmth on those chilly spring mornings. On the other hand, if I get hot, the sleeves zip off and can be easily rolled up and placed into one of the many pockets in the vest. The vest also has a very thick cushioned seat that has become more important the older I have become. Comfort and camouflage mean a lot when you have to wait a long time on ole tom.

A few seasons back, I was talking about turkey hunting with my son when an elderly friend of ours overheard the conversation. She enthusiastically made mention of the turkeys she was seeing *every* morning behind her house. Naturally, this got my curiosity going and I proceeded to ask for permission to hunt her property. She granted permission without any problem. Needless to say, the very next morning I found myself listening to several toms gobbling from the roost located at the edge of a bean field. After flying down from the roost, the turkeys proceeded to feed into the bean field. This particular field had not been planted yet, but was still covered with bean stubble from the previous harvest. Two mature gobblers, one jake and four hens fed their way across the field. The field itself was bordered on two sides by fencerows and covered about fifty acres.

I watched the turkeys through my binoculars trying to decide how I was going to hunt them. I decided to wait until they fed into a low spot in the landscape and then I would make my move. The plan was to get ahead of them and hide in the fencerow where I might get a shot at one as they fed past my hideout. I had already killed six turkeys by hunting in multiple states and really wanted to finish out the season with seven.

After the turkeys fed into the low spot, I headed for my intended location. There was only one flaw in my plan, the field was bigger than I had anticipated and before I could get to the other side, one of the gobblers fed onto a rise in the landscape. There I stood—busted! The only thing I could do was stand as still as possible and see what happened. My face was covered by the head net. The gobbler was still three hundred yards away and I elected to slowly melt into a crouching position.

This particular day was rather windy and the leaves on my hunting vest were blowing in the breeze. At three hundred yards that ole tom lifted up his head and stared at me for eternity. Then, he curiously started walking straight toward me. He didn't waste any time doing so and I think he had fighting on his mind.

The next thing I knew, that ole turkey had walked two hundred yards straight to me with only one hundred to go. I fully expected him to stop at any moment, raise his head, and cautiously walk in the opposite direction. On the contrary, he kept right on coming. About seventy-five yards out, the gobbler walked into a low spot that obscured his sight from me. I quickly fell to my belly and positioned my gun for the shot. The next time he came into view, the turkey was thirty-five yards from the end of my barrel. Seconds later, he was flopping with my foot on his head.

For what it's worth—I owe the leaves sewn onto my hunting vest for killing that ole gobbler. I am convinced the synthetic leaves were blowing in the breeze. In a crouched position, I looked like a strutting gobbler to my wary quarry. I don't think it would ever happen again, but stranger things have happened (although I can't imagine what they might be).

My elderly lady friend watched the entire episode from her kitchen window and got quite a thrill from it all. She stated she had never seen anyone call a turkey from such a distance to which I responded, "me neither."

Challenge: Breezy days can make many things appear differently—especially at a distance. The winds of time can also make *people* appear different than they really are. The outer shell looks battered and worn, but they are the same on the inside. Are you guilty of treating others differently because they are older? If you look into the eyes of an elderly person, you will often see a younger person dying to get out. They still have the same feelings and personality they have always had. What they really need is the younger generation to understand them. The outside appearance can be deceiving. Stop looking at the elderly from a distance. Get to know them up close and personally and you will see them for who they *really* are.

Thought: You can change the way you appear on the outside and fool many. But only God can change you on the inside.

A gray head is a crown of glory.   *Proverbs 16:31*

For wisdom is better than jewels and all desirable things cannot compare with her.   *Proverbs 8:11*

The First Turkey Hunt

I love to take people on their first turkey hunt. They really do not know what to expect. Most of the time, the hunt doesn't turn out like the videos we see depicting the strutting gobbler that comes running to investigate the decoys. Videos usually do not show the time it takes to find a willing tom and call him into gun range. Of the turkeys I have killed, very few have come to my calling directly from the roost. Neither have most of the birds I have been fortunate enough to bag been "easy." These birds have required my utmost in skill and determination to finally sling them over my shoulder.

It is the difficulty of the hunt that breeds respect for the quarry. If turkeys were easy to kill, everyone would be turkey hunting and there wouldn't be many birds left to pursue. Those of us who enter the woods each spring to chase longbeards know how difficult to kill these birds can often become. As a result, it is my intention to teach respect for the bird we hunt as much as hunting or calling skills to the rookie hunter. However, there are sometimes when I enjoy playing with the naiveté of the beginning hunter as evidenced by the following story.

When I lived in West Virginia, Mike Evans, a pharmaceutical representative from Tennessee, and I would schedule a few hunts each spring. Mike had never killed a turkey and was eagerly interested in learning the ropes of the sport. Mike was in his early thirties at the time and greatly anticipated killing his first bird. Without a doubt, he was one of the nicest people I have ever met. Why he chose me to be his mentor puzzles me to this day. But one thing is for sure—we had some interesting experiences together.

Mike is the only other person I have met who has had a bird land on his body. We were sitting in an old road awaiting daylight. As the morning awoke and the sky began to lighten, a small bird flew from a thicket and landed on Mike's shoulder. I suppose the 3-D camo Mike wore with branches overlying two layers of leaves fooled even the bird's eyes. That little sparrow actually thought he was landing on a twig. Just goes to show you how good the camo is today. I wouldn't have believed it had it not happened before my very eyes. In fact, that bird almost landed on me as well.

On one of our first hunts, Mike and I walked for a mile or more to the top of a small mountain. At the top of the mountain was a grassy field and I suspected turkeys would be using this area although I had never heard one gobble from that location. Sometimes spring in the mountains of West Virginia is forever in coming. It was difficult listening to my buddies in Tennessee and other southern states talk of hearing turkeys gobble when I was still contending with snow and other wet, cold weather.

This particular morning was cold, wet, and foggy. I was hoping to get Mike on a bird but the weather was not cooperating. I decided to walk around the edges of the field and call down into the valleys below hoping to raise a gobble. After we had walked around the field without success, we were slowly walking across the field to return to the truck when I noticed something moving just inside the woods. Mike and I both had our head nets donned. Upon seeing the movement, I immediately whispered for Mike to "freeze."

The movement was a mature gobbler cruising the edge of the field looking for the hen he had heard minutes before. All I could see was his white head bouncing along the edge of the field. He was about seventy-five yards from our position. I whispered to Mike, "no matter what I do, don't move—just stand still."

The turkey was maintaining his direction and continuing just inside the tree line. There we stood in the middle of the field without cover of any kind except the thin blanket of fog still present. I noticed a big poplar tree ahead of the tom. If he continued on his present course, he would walk directly behind that old poplar tree. I decided to gamble for a shot—after all, we were *so* busted.

When the gobbler's head was totally concealed by the big poplar, I took off in a dead run directly toward the tree. While running, I was mentally calculating the turkey's movement behind the tree and compensated for the angle at which I needed to stay in order to stay hidden from the turkey's view. After running some thirty yards, I quickly dropped down on one knee and raised my gun. When the turkey's head popped out on the other side of the big poplar, my gun roared.

Mike came hurriedly to the spot where the turkey's wings were beating the ground (I love that sound) and said, "Man, that was awesome!" I casually responded, "Mike, I'm glad you were here to watch this hunt— *that* is the way you kill 'em." "Cool," was his response.

Before the next spring rolled around, we moved to Kentucky. To this day, almost ten years later, Mike *still* has not killed a turkey. He is now married and has children. He is no longer a pharmaceutical representative. Life has changed. Yet, in the springtime, the constant allure of killing a wild turkey still keeps him awake at night.

Sometimes, I feel guilty and sometimes I snicker to myself. Sometimes, I feel the need to call ole Mike and set the record straight. Other times, I reason, "Sometimes, you just have to learn things the hard way." Mike has never been able to run down ole tom like I did on that foggy morning. If you happen to be hunting in eastern Tennessee and see someone running madly toward your jake decoy, don't get too upset, it's really not *his* fault. The boy never learned any differently. He is the product of the one who trained him.

Challenge: How well are you training your sons, daughters, or friends to pursue the wild turkey? How well are you training them to pursue God?

Thought: The student will become exactly like his teacher. Are you a mentor worth copying?

A pupil is not above his teacher; but everyone, after he has been fully trained, will be like his teacher. Luke 6:40

The Lost Art

There is something to be said for all the new technology available today. However, there is also a down side. Our western lifestyle is so fast paced that life whirls by at the speed of light and the desire for instant gratification in every sector of life is crowding out the virtue of patience. Yet, beneath this wave of fast food chains, pre-fabricated houses, and continuous busyness is a foundation of simplicity. It has always been there but has been silenced amid the cries of greed, selfishness, and carefree living.

Prior to the industrial revolution, Americans taught their young ladies the domestic skills needed to support family life and young men were taught trades whereby they could provide for their families. It seems this instantaneous culture in which we live seeks to skip the basics in order to "get to the good stuff."

Without solid foundations, houses would not stand. Without basic mathematics, computers would crash. Without basic principles of ethics and consideration, people become a bunch of "me, myself, and I's." Our entire culture seems to be spinning out of control without regard for the consequences of a self-absorbed society. We have forgotten where we have come from and consequently do not know where we are headed. Wherever we *are* going—we are getting there fast.

Fifty years from now, how many stands of hardwoods will be left? Will our timber industry be sold out completely to other nations? How much of our water will be polluted? How much of the now rolling farmland will be covered with housing subdivisions? Will hunting and fishing still be preserved for those of us who have found such delight in them? Will America's open policy toward immigration eventually weaken our historical identity to the extent lawmakers who do not share our background take away the right to keep and bear arms? Answers to these questions and many more will largely be determined in the future by what we sportsman do today.

I am not a proponent of sticking one's head in the sand and pretending these things are not happening. However, there is something about escaping to the wilds with primitive equipment in hand that reminds me of a simpler day. A day when the boundaries of life and death were not nearly as blurred and one had to acknowledge them in order to survive. I am talking about food, water, shelter, clothing, weather, and interpersonal relationships. One depended upon the woods, water, and soil to produce the basic needs of life and the help of friends to preserve them. Today, it seems everything is plastic and mechanical. Traffic jams and meat wrapped in cellophane are the norm.

I know you can't hold back the tide of modernization and technological advancement is here to stay. But this ole boy hopes to experience as much of the country as possible before it becomes extinct. Although I love the western states and the vast number of acres now permanently saved from encroachment of civilization, this is not the "country" to which I am referring. I applaud and support the work of the NRA, Rocky Mountain Elk Foundation, and NWTF. But the "country" to which I am referring has not been purchased or managed by these organizations. I am referring to the "country" right here in my backyard. The places I have hunted for twenty years but have now lost the rights to hunt. Owners have died and land has been sold or transferred to relatives making it difficult to continue hunting the same old jaunts. Land that used to be available for hunting is now usually leased by clubs—making it even harder to find a hunting spot. Public hunting areas can sometimes be crowded or spoiled by the presence of human scent.

Watching hunting land disappear or become unavailable is a heartbreak indeed. I remember as a young boy listening to men who were in their mid-forties talk about how things had changed since they were younger and that trend has only escalated. It is not going to stop. So what is a man supposed to do? Either invest in your own land, or do the best you can with what you have all the while teaching the next generation to be a good steward with the land that *is* available.

In some ways, the above descriptions depict what the American Indians (at least in part) must have felt like. I suppose that is why I like to hunt with "primitive" equipment. Although, the equipment I use is still more technologically advanced than the bows and arrows of the American Indian, there is still a romance found in using a stick, string, and wooden arrow shaft.

Several years ago, I decided to make my own arrows using cedar shafts and turkey feathers from the previous spring's harvest. I remember staining, dipping and cresting my favored shafts in preparation for bow season. During that season, the aromatic smell of broken cedar reminded me of the thrill of success. Walking up to a downed animal that has been harvested with primitive equipment and instinctive shooting skills awakens the senses to a period since lost. It is my fear our society is losing the connection to the simplicity of its past.

It may be old-fashioned to believe domestic and trade skills are still needed to build a healthy home. But I for one believe in laying foundations of simplicity. If we do not take time to lay a solid foundation, then whatever we build in life will surely come tumbling down during the first big storm that comes along. By "simplicity" I am referring to the basics necessary for a culture to survive. Things like self-respect, a strong work ethic, integrity, honesty, patience, unselfishness, and a sense of mutual accountability both to God and our fellow man.

So it is with hunting, we must train the next generation to understand and appreciate the simple foundations of western civilization. Secondly, we must teach them to be good stewards with the "country" that is now left. Thirdly, we must teach them how to cope with ever changing expansion and equip them with the ability to preserve all the "country" they possibly can. The next generation must recover the lost art of simplicity before Americans forget where they came from—for we must appreciate where we have come from in order to understand where we are going.

Challenge: In your chronic busyness, have you lost touch with the simplicities of life? List five things you can do to simplify your lifestyle. How much time are you spending developing the basic simplicities of knowing God: reading His Word, listening to Him, talking with Him, and obeying Him?

Thought: Don't forget where His grace has brought you *from* or you will lose sight of where He wants you to go.

> *But I am afraid, lest as the serpent deceived Eve by his craftiness, your minds should be led astray from the simplicity and purity of devotion to Christ.*
> 2 Corinthians 11:3

Warriors

Every now and then, for those who have eyes to see, the natural things God has so delicately created can teach us invaluable lessons and show us the intricate details of His creative genius. Each summer along the fencerows of our farm, a strange little vine grows yielding what is called the Passion Flower. When I was a kid we called them "maypops" to describe the green pod filled with tangy seeds that grows on the vine. The Passion Flower is without a doubt one of the most ornately detailed flowers I have ever seen. I can't help but study one of them when they are in bloom. They simply amaze me. Yet this "weed" is often sprayed without thought for its beauty or regard for the designer's details. I wonder how many other beautiful displays of God's glory go unnoticed by the average outdoorsman?

Most of us are not dendrologist or ornithologist. Our knowledge of the trees, birds, or plants are not vast but enough to understand nature and how it works. While I can tell many different species from another, I cannot tell you the scientific name or genus to which they belong. But it is enough for me to simply draw lessons for life by observing the handiwork of God's creation.

I know many of the birds by sound and by name, but there is one little bird for which I do not know the name. I don't know if it is a cowbird or what. But it is a bold little creature. I often see this little bird and sometimes more than one, attacking hawks, crows, or buzzards with bulldog tenacity. These little birds sweep onto the backs of the larger birds and just annoy them to death. I don't know their names but I do know their cause. Regardless of whether they are trying to keep these larger birds away from their nests or just love to aggravate them, their cause is to completely drive larger birds out of the area. And they are not afraid of wingspan, power, or the flying ability of those they oppose. What is to keep a hawk from teaching these little dive-bombers a lesson? They are certainly no match for the hawk's razor sharp talons. No sir, these little black birds are fearless or perhaps they have more to live for than themselves.

What is it that has made men and women lay down their lives for "the greater cause" throughout history? Many of these courageous warriors have lost their lives for the expansion of political empires, the greed of men, or to oppose tyranny. Some have lost their lives while seeking to protect their family and friends or the freedom they and others enjoy.

The one who follows Christ must fight against the flesh, sin, Satan, and the world. We are called to be warriors. But the main fight the Word of God calls us to enter is the "good fight of faith." It is in the arena of faith that men either stand or fall. The forces of this world either cut us down immediately or bleed the life out of us in a slow agonizing death. Anyone who has been scarred by the financial, political, or administrative blows of this world can testify to the fierceness of the battle called life. Life can often be empty and meaningless without a "greater cause" and in this case a "greater person" to live for than ourselves. Christ is our victor and soon coming King. He is the commander-in-chief and He is the one who calls our faith to trust Him with the outcome of our lives.

Just like the aforementioned birds, we should not shrink back from those who seek to destroy our faith but run boldly into the battle casting intimidation and fear aside. We should attack the fortresses of our enemy with constancy and determination without regard for personal safety. And when it comes time for us to die, people may not know our names, but they *will* remember our cause.

Challenge: Are you fighting in the right arena for the right cause or wasting your energy fighting the wrong battles for the wrong reasons?

Thought: Your life's emotional, mental, spiritual, and physical scars will tell the tale of the battles you fought.

Therefore I run in such a way, as not without aim; I box in such a way, as not beating the air... 1 Corinthians 9:26

For though we walk in the flesh, we do not war according to the flesh, for the weapons of our warfare are not of the flesh, but divinely powerful for the destruction of fortresses.
2 Corinthians 10:3-4

Fight the good fight of faith... 1 Timothy 6:12

What's All the Buzz About?

Spring is the grandest time of the year. Nature comes alive with its many sights and sounds. Butterflies, frogs, and birds all make it known they are glad to be alive. Have you ever stopped to ponder the intricate and almost unbelievable characteristics of the wild world we take so much for granted? For instance, the hummingbird's wings beat thirty-three times every time the second hand ticks. That represents an amazing speed. Mathematically speaking, it is impossible for a bumblebee to fly due to the smallness of its wings, yet they fly with incredible agility and speed. Consider the honeybee. The hive has three types of bees—the queen, drones, and workers. The queen bee mates with one of thousands of drones in mid-air flight. Once she mates with the drone, he dies. She is then capable of laying thousands of eggs to produce other bees. Once pollen is located, the worker bees come back to the hive and perform an aerobatic dance that tells the other worker bees where the pollen is located. These guys have a built-in compass that navigates by the sun and therefore always know how to get back to the hive. Worker bees only live for about a month and literally wear out their wings serving their queen.

There are many life applications to learn from nature if one ponders the evidence of God's creative hand throughout. For instance, consider the birds. They were never meant to stay in the nest as evidenced by a mother eagle's removing the soft plumage from her nest when its time for her eaglets to learn to fly. Furthermore, it is the nature of birds to fly and they are eager to learn. Therefore, it is fitting to say a parent is to train his child to fly. That is, to train children to aim high and do their best at life no matter what. In so doing, kids learn to rise to any occasion that tests their mettle. Yet, many parents are not conscientious of this fact and rarely work at giving their children wings much less teaching them how to use them.

Personally, it is not enough to teach my kids to merely fly. I want to teach them how to soar. If kids learn to soar above every circumstance of life, they see things from a heavenly perspective and are able to overcome any obstacle in their path. They will be able to rise above their problems and see them differently than the average person who simply knows how to fly away from their problems. Yet, like a cat on the prowl, the problem continues to pursue and kids who habitually fly away will never escape their problems.

Consider the worker bee. Am I willing to totally spend life serving my King? Like the worker bee, at the end of my life, will I collapse with exhaustion? Will I fall at the feet of Jesus having given him all I had to offer thus fulfilling His purpose for my life?

Like the bumblebee, when people say something is "impossible," will I continue in faith believing God's word anyway? Will I soar with God against insurmountable odds while the naysayers tell me something cannot be done? Will I prove God to be the God of impossibilities? The blind are not supposed to see—but some do. The lame are not supposed to walk—but some do. The deaf are not supposed to hear—but some do. God can do anything He chooses to do. And He can do the impossible through you and me.

If we can learn to *study* nature instead of merely *observe* it, spiritual applications are everywhere and this is the key to loving God with all of your consciousness. Don't be surprised when sharing your insights with others that some may not understand. Loving and experiencing God in this manner is a learned and conscious response to God's creative handiwork. The average person doesn't see it. For some of us, it may occur naturally, but for others it does not.

It is also important to note that observations concerning nature must coincide with God's truth in the Word of God—the Bible. For many desire to have their eyes opened to nature, but not according to *God's* truth and therefore leave themselves vulnerable to mere human intellect and rationale. Although *some* truth may be discovered in this manner, it is not the kind of life-changing truth that accompanies God's perspective. These people have a tendency to worship nature itself. For this reason, the follower of Christ asks the Holy Spirit to reveal the lessons taught through nature. Therefore, the applications learned through creation lead us to *the Creator Himself*. This is of paramount importance when learning to listen to God's voice through observing creation.

Challenge: When is the last time you stopped to ponder the millions of things God has created to continually point us to Him?

Thought: The old phrase, "familiarity breeds contempt" is true when it comes to taking what God has created for granted.

Open my eyes, that I may behold wonderful things from Thy law.
Psalm 119:18

For since the creation of the world His invisible attributes, His eternal power and divine nature, have been clearly seen, being understood through what has been made, so that they are without excuse.
Romans 1:20

Fruitfulness

I was born in the heartland of Mississippi and grew up in a small county seat town. While there was a small amount of farming that occurred within our community, most people were not row crop farmers. And while it is certainly true that regions in Mississippi contain vast farmlands, I did not grow up among them. Therefore, farming was not something I experienced regularly on a large scale.

My wife, on the other hand, grew up in the west central part of Kentucky where farming is *big* business. Little did I know we would someday make our way back to her old stomping grounds and eventually have a farm of our own. I have always loved the smell of dirt (except while running with a football) and enjoyed watching things grow. Therefore, it has been a satisfying experience for me to plant food plots for the game that runs around on our farm. I have enjoyed providing the practical needs of these animals as much as I have hunting them.

After moving to Kentucky, I was impressed with the topography and the beauty of the land. Patterning the movements of wildlife seemed much easier than in Mississippi where hunting deer with dogs is still a grand tradition. I don't have a problem with hunting with dogs, but for me, I would rather hunt game in a natural environment when they are not running for *deer* life.

In Kentucky as in Mississippi, a lot of the timber has been cut to clear land for farming. Therefore, if a hunter locates a tract of timber large enough to hunt, there is usually cropland nearby. As a result, feeding and bedding areas are not hard to locate. On one farm, I could tell exactly what the deer would do every year. This advantage was awesome since deer movements could be easily predicted without the need for scouting and spreading human scent throughout the area. Over a period of years, I bagged many deer from that area. Three of the deer heads now hanging on my wall were taken within one hundred fifty yards of one another. And I saw or missed several bucks within the same area larger than these.

One of the things that impressed me about Kentucky was the vastness of the farm fields. While driving to my hunting destination, I would literally see miles and miles of wheat, corn, or soybeans. One afternoon while making my way to a favorite deer stand, I began pondering the many ears of corn being produced by one seed of corn. The results were amazing. Each kernel of corn had produced hundreds of times over. Kernels had produced ears of corn that produced bushels of corn that produced bins filled with corn—tons of corn.

How fitting and proper the analogies of Jesus as he walked through the fields with his disciples. Jesus often talked about this miracle of multiplication using the examples of crops, fruit, and seeds. I was walking amidst one of the most concrete examples of Jesus' command to multiply His work in our lives. The truth of Jesus' teaching struck me profoundly. From then on, I could no longer see the beauty of these vast crop lands without whispering a silent prayer—"Lord, may my life be as fruitful as these fields for your glory."

Challenge: What kind of fruit is your life producing?

Thought: The kind of seed you and others sow into your life will determine the fruit you produce. Weeds and thorns come to seed on their own.

Truly, truly, I say to you, unless a grain of wheat falls into the earth and dies, it remains by itself alone; but if it dies, it bears much fruit. He who loves his life loses it; and he who hates his life in this world shall keep it to life eternal.   John 12:24-25

Now the parable is this: the seed is the word of God. And those beside the road are those who have heard; then the devil comes and takes away the word from their heart, so that they may not believe and be saved. And those on the rocky soil are those who, when

they hear, receive the word with joy; and these have no firm root;
they believe for a while, and in time of temptation fall away. And
the seed which fell among the thorns, these are the ones who have
heard, and as they go on their way they are choked with worries and
riches and pleasures of this life, and bring no fruit to maturity. And
the seed in the good soil, these are the ones who have heard the word
in an honest and good heart, and hold it fast, and bear fruit with
perseverance.   *Luke 8:11-15*

Timing is Everything

I had finished the morning's turkey hunt only to discover my truck had not one but *two* flat tires. What are the chances of having *two* flats at the same time? No, I hadn't run through a batch of nails scattered upon the road. The culprits turned out to be small shards of flint from the gravel road on which I had been parked. After calling a friend of mine, we fixed the tires and I headed home. During the drive home, the clouds grew dark and rain appeared to be coming my way. While driving past one of my favorite "turkey fields," I noticed three long beards feeding in the field. After driving past the turkeys, I quickly turned around and parked my vehicle. The field was owned by a friend of mine's cousin so I wasn't concerned about trespassing since I had permission to hunt this particular property.

As I made my way toward the field, I could see the gobbler feeding about ninety yards out in the field. Ever so slowly, I crept closer and closer. One of the gobblers had a twelve-inch beard and I fixed my determined will on bagging him. I wasn't familiar with the lay of the land and came to a point where I could not get any closer without being detected.

During the stalk, the wind started blowing around forty miles per hour and the clouds spilled gallons of water upon my head. I quickly became a wet blob of camouflage. Suddenly, the thunderstorm exchanged the water for ice as hail began to fall in torrents. I had experienced this phenomenon before while turkey hunting but wasn't prepared for what would happen next. Surprisingly, when the hail started falling, all three gobblers placed their heads under their wing as thunder boomed and lightening flashed. Now I had my chance to kill that ole long beard, *but* I hesitated. The turkeys kept their heads under their wing for a full two minutes before they started heading toward the corner of the field. I had missed my opportunity.

I continued to pursue the turkeys for another two hours but never connected. I learned an important lesson during that stalk and yet I have
never seen another turkey tuck his head under his wing in such fashion.
When you get an opportunity like the one I just described and fail to take
advantage of it, usually the result is a blank tag and an empty plate—a
painful reminder of words from my high school chemistry teacher, "He
who hesitates is lost."

Another such event occurred during a bow hunt for whitetails. I had
purchased a recurve from the local pawnshop to see if traditional hunting
was for me. After ordering a dozen cedar arrows and a few broadheads,
I dreamed of bow hunting all summer as I practiced for the moment of
truth. As it turned out, my experience with a recurve turned out to be a
romance from the beginning. Prior to the opening day of season, I con-
structed several ladder stands made of treated lumber and placed them
on several well-used deer trails. Bagging any deer with recurve equipment
would be considered a trophy.

Finally, the day came and I found myself sitting aloft the ladder stand
watching over a well-used deer run. The stand was only twelve feet high
and the trail itself was uphill from the stand. Therefore, I knew my eleva-
tion was marginal at best to actually get off a shot. As experience predicted, around 8:00 a.m. a young doe made her way toward my stand and
just as I started to draw my bow—she looked directly at me. All I could
do was freeze and silently chide myself for setting up in this manner.

Without explanation, a gray squirrel started descending a tree a few
feet from the stand. As he made his way down, he started barking at
the young doe and making all kinds of racket. For a brief moment, the
deer was distracted and started watching the squirrel instead of me.
Remembering the lesson I had learned while hunting turkeys in the hail-
storm, I slowly drew my bow and in one fluid motion released the arrow.
At the twang of the string, the young deer's head snapped in my direction but the arrow had already ripped through her ribcage. As she spun
around to head in the direction from which she had come, I knew I had

just harvested my second deer using a recurve. A lesson well learned produced a plate well adorned with succulent venison.

Challenge: Can you remember a mistake while hunting that has made you a better hunter? Did you learn from it? In the same vein, have your mistakes throughout life helped you become a better person? Do you continue to make the same mistakes again and again or do you learn from them?

Thoughts: There are moments in life when we dare not hesitate to make a decision, otherwise we will miss the opportunity. On the other hand, some decisions need to be made through prudence and careful calculation. Either way, it is important to base our decisions upon the wisdom of God. Do you consult Him regularly in the decision making process? If not, why not? Ask someone to help you if needed. You wouldn't hesitate to help someone if they were having problems with hunting, would you? Neither will a true believer in God hesitate to help you. Ask.

If any of you lacks wisdom, let him ask of God, who gives to all men generously and without reproach, and it will be given to him.

James 1:5

The Log

Every time I have walked across a log to get to the other side of a stream, I have wondered if the log was actually strong enough to hold my weight. Sometimes the smaller logs are stronger than the larger ones. It simply depends upon the type of tree and how long it has been down. I have a lot of outdoor memories relating to logs and dead trees.

One such experience with logs occurred during a spring gobbler hunt in Mississippi. Mark Sandifer and I were hunting alongside a creek. A gobbler was sounding off from the roost on the other side. We quickly made our way to the foot log since we had crossed there many times before. I had noticed on the last several crossings that the old log was becoming increasingly weak. Before we started to cross the log, I told Mark to allow me to cross first since the log would not hold both of us. "Oh, yes it will. This log is huge and has been here forever. It can handle both of us at the same time," he replied. "No, it won't—just trust me," was my response.

After having said that, I started across the big log. When I was three quarters of the way across, Mark decided to give it a try. Immediately, that familiar cracking sound occurred. You know, that sound when wood *breaks*. I knew time was of the essence and very quickly lurched for the opposite bank. Just as my hand wrapped around a small sapling, a deafening noise sent a shockwave rippling through the morning stillness. The entire makeshift bridge collapsed into the current below leaving only my left boot a little wet. Mark, on the other hand, was not as fortunate.

After quickly climbing the bank, I frantically searched for Mark. All I could see was Mark's hat floating on the surface of the creek. We had fished together many times and I knew Mark to be a good swimmer. However, I wasn't sure what had happened to him during the fall. My concern quickly abated when I saw Mark's head break the surface of the creek. The coldness of the water had taken his breath away and he came forth gasping for air. Concern turned to humor as I realized Mark was standing. He was okay. What can I say? He should have listened!

Another memory involves Kenny Williams' attempt to bounce me into a small creek one cold spring morning. I was to cross the log first and then Kenny would follow. Experience had taught me Kenny was unpredictable when it came to pranks and careless curiosity. On one particular hunt, he started pushing on a dead snag and it came crashing down to the forest floor. Luckily, neither of us was knocked unconscious by the falling debris.

I carefully made the tightrope walk across the small log. Halfway across the log and in the middle of the creek, additional vibrations alerted me Kenny had climbed upon the log also. He started snickering and bouncing up and down in an effort to throw me into the creek—some friend, huh? I remember thinking, "If I can just keep my balance, then maybe he will fall instead of me." Much to my pleasure, things grew silent for a brief moment before the splash. With the grace and balance of a trapeze artist, I made my way to the other side and immediately found a seat whereby to tease and laugh at my shivering buddy.

I suppose using logs as footbridges is as old as nature itself. Every now and then, someone tries to come up with something new. You know, a sort of—"I can do better than this attitude." Kenny Williams is one of those people who is always thinking of ways to improve things. Now, I am not saying this is a bad thing. Believe me, it's great to have a thinker in the group when you run into trouble. But there is never a good reason to re-invent the wheel—so it goes with creek crossings.

Kenny told me one day, "Suppose you need to get to that ole gobbler across the creek and you can't find a log across the creek. You don't want to be soaking wet the rest of the day, so you pull out two large trash bags, pull them over your boots and legs and walk on across." That solution sounded good to ole Kenny and he promptly loaded his turkey vest with two large trash bags in case such a situation presented itself. Sure enough, a few weeks later, Kenny needed to get to a gobbling bird on the other side of a small creek. There was no fallen log to be found. As he reached for his homemade waders, Kenny realized he only had one bag instead of two. Apparently, he had lost one of them on a previous outing.

Not to be outdone by the situation, Kenny started thinking of a way to beat the system. He reasoned to himself, "If I can just pull this bag over both legs at the same time, I can shuffle my feet and inch my way across the creek." And that he did. Things were progressing well and Kenny was congratulating himself for developing such a lightweight, commonsensical solution to the problem. However, when Kenny reached the middle of the small creek, things began to go south. The current of the creek began to push between Kenny's legs as the bag began to function like a large underwater sail. Kenny struggled to maintain his balance but the current eventually won the battle. In disappointing surrender, Kenny's legs gave way to the current and were swept out from under him. Down the would-be inventor went into the chill of the cold water.

The last time a turkey gobbled on the other side of a creek from Kenny, I watched him wade immediately across and keep right on hunting. I guess he figured, "If you are going to get wet anyway, there is no sense putting it off!"

Challenge: Are you helping others get to the other side of problems, difficulties, and failures or making fun of them while secretly hoping they will fall? This question holds true in business, athletics, recreation, and life.

Thoughts: There is only one tree bridging from here to heaven and it is the cross of Jesus. People are constantly trying to figure out a way to "beat the system" but there is no other way. Jesus is the *only* way to the other side. All other religious bridges will surely collapse no matter how old and well used they may be.

For God so loved the world, that He gave His only begotten Son, that whoever believes in Him should not perish, but have eternal life. For God did not send the Son into the world to judge the world, but that the world should be saved through Him.

John 3:16-17

No Shoulders

As a young boy, I was deathly afraid of snakes. One friend of mine called them "no shoulders." Living in the deep South, snakes were a normal occurrence. Sometimes while duck hunting, we would see cottonmouth water moccasins in the middle of winter. However, my good friends Jonathan and Daniel Carraway helped me overcome this fear when I was a teenager. I will never forget the first time I caught a snake with my bare hands. This one episode relinquished my fear of snakes. However, to say I *like* snakes would be far from the truth. Suffice to say, I have a healthy respect for the vipers that are poisonous. As long as I can see them, everything is fine. Snakes of the rattling type that hide in the weeds unnerve me to this day. Fortunately, that has happened only a couple of times.

Most of the time, snakes are not a problem and there is no telling how many I have passed by without being aware of their presence. I have seen some monster snakes in my day and have several large timber rattlesnake skins in my trophy room exceeding six feet in length. Yet, if the truth were known, I would rather leave them to themselves. In spite of my best efforts at getting over this phobia, sometimes, I hear stories like the following that make me shiver.

My friend, Jay Ellis, was hunting in the Mississippi Delta. Now, for those of you unfamiliar with the Mississippi Delta region, it is known for growing big things—kinda like Texas. In the past, the delta has been known for its big farming fields, fish ponds, and growing large deer as well as harboring millions of ducks each year. And let's not forget its legendary status as a snake producer as well as the reputation for producing huge, kamikaze mosquitoes.

Jay was bow hunting one afternoon and was climbing a steep bank that arose out of a swamp. As he made his way up the bank, Jay felt something swipe past his hair just above the ear. Coming into focus at eye level was a large rattlesnake that had just struck at Jay's head. Jay quickly reacted by falling backward down the bank and rolling to a stop. Immediately, he was met with the unnerving sound of rattling. He had stopped his descent from the bank right beside another rattler! Jay instinctively rolled away from the snake with blazing speed escaping the snake's strike.

After returning to his feet, Jay ran away from the area as mud and water almost sucked the boots from his feet. After tiring from his rapid yet narrow escape, Jay decided to sit down on an old log for a brief rest. His panic had almost subsided as he processed the events that had taken place. Thank God, he was safe.

While sitting on the log, much to Jay's horror, his eyes caught a flash of white. Beside the log on which he was sitting was a cottonmouth water moccasin. The snake had already opened its white mouth to warn Jay of its intentions if he were to get any closer. Jay quickly spun away from the snake and hurriedly made his way back to his vehicle. I guess some fellows don't have to be actually bitten by a snake to be "snake bit."

Challenge: Have you ever wondered how many times God has protected you when you were completely unaware of the danger around you? What about the times when you *were* aware of the danger around you? Did you express gratitude for His supernatural protection?

Thought: The next time you have a close brush with death, thank the One who has saved you. When life becomes uncertain—run to Him.

In the Lord I take refuge...   *Psalm 11:1*

The name of the Lord is a strong tower; the righteous run into it and are safe.   *Proverbs 18:10*

He who dwells in the shelter of the Most High will abide in the shadow of the Almighty. I will say to the Lord, "My refuge and my fortress, My God, in whom I trust!" For it is He who delivers you from the snare of the trapper, and from the deadly pestilence.

Psalm 91:1-3

Neglect

I'm not a large-scale farmer. In fact, I am still learning how to plant food plots for wildlife and enough vegetables to feed our family of six. However, I have learned there are many enemies to the would-be farmer—insects, drought, floods, and weeds just to name a few. Weeds would rank number one on my list since they will grow no matter what. There are particular weeds that really give the dirt lover problems with regard to the pain it takes to get rid of them.

I remember as a young teen hearing Billy Hillman complain about "thistle." Billy was a forester and walked the fields bordering the woods quite often. One day I asked him why he sometimes wore leg chaps. He responded by stating, "Someday, I will show you." That day came sooner than I had anticipated.

It was time to load the small boat into the back of the truck and head for the fishin' hole. Billy and I loved to fish those out of the way places that no one else seemed to notice. Small creeks that wound through large woodlots seemed to be our favorite—no big motors or fancy gear—just a paddle, tackle box and a few poles. We often fished with live bait that made these fishing escapades quite an adventure. It seemed to me this was the way fishing was supposed to be—quiet, cool, and fun. We almost always filled our stringer with fish.

On one particular outing as described above, we decided the best place to slide the boat into the water was adjacent to a small field bordering the creek. One thing we had not anticipated was the grown up field being covered in thistle. Both of us were wearing shorts and it was almost impossible to move without getting poked and pricked by one of those dastardly plants. By the time we got the boat into the water, both of us were in a bad mood due to the battle with our relentless foe.

It has been a long time since that day and I now live in the middle of row crop country. Farming is all around me. I quickly notice groups of thistle growing on the side of the road or in someone else's neglected field and other farmers notice them as well. Why so much fuss over a weed? Because thistles spread seed by the millions. These seeds are spread by riding the currents of the wind. Therefore, if one farmer does not deal with his thistles, they become another farmer's problem. Consequently, it is kind of an unspoken rule that each farmer does not allow this potential problem to get out of control on his farm. If you do, the neighboring farmers will not be happy.

Now, you might be saying, "why don't you just spray the pesky things?" Well, it's not that easy. Yes, we do spray them. But you have to spray every single plant for the spray to be effective and sometimes when spot spraying, it is easy to miss the little plants. Consequently, they continue growing and if one is not diligent to spray another round, the second generation of thistles is born. When stumbling across one or two thistle plants (missed by spraying), older farmers usually remove them by the roots. If you merely cut the plant down, it will often sprout again and still bear seeds.

It takes a lot of persistent determination to get rid of thistles and stay rid of thistles. And yet, they still manage to come back year after year. If left alone, they will literally take over a field. Each time I have noticed a field full of thistle, my thoughts have wondered about the overseer of the field. What is he thinking? Is he still alive? What are the neighboring farmers thinking?

The truth is—one cannot kill every single thistle plant. However, if the tender of the soil pays very close attention, he can practically neutralize the threat of losing his farm to thistles. It simply takes a consistent, bulldog determination to win the battle.

Challenge: The next time you see thistles growing in a neglected field, remind yourself of the constant need to keep you own heart free from sin. If you do not, you will surely be overtaken by the evil that comes to seed on its own.

Thoughts: The seeds of your life are blowing into the lives of others. Are you sowing blessings or curses for generations that follow? You are also the product of someone else sowing seed into your life. Who are the people that have sown positive seed into your life verses those who have sown negative seed into your life? How do you think people would rank you in terms of your impact upon them?

> *Do not be deceived, God is not mocked; for whatever a man sows; this he will also reap. For the one who sows to his own flesh shall from the flesh reap corruption, but the one who sows to the Spirit shall from the Spirit reap eternal life.* Galatians 6:7-8

> *For the ground that drinks the rain which often falls upon it and brings forth vegetation useful to those for whose sake it is also tilled, receives a blessing from God; but if it yields thorns and thistles, it is worthless and close to being cursed, and it ends up being burned.* Hebrews 6:7-8

> *And I passed by the field of the lazy, and by the vineyard of the man lacking sense; and behold, it was completely overgrown with thistles, Its surface was covered with nettles, And its stone wall was broken down.* Proverbs 24:30-31

This is what a man's life looks like to others when he neglects to keep his heart clean before God. Jesus teaches us to deal ruthlessly with our sin— pull it out by the roots!

Seasons of Reflection

How Can I Know God?

God created us to love and serve Him. In the beginning, man had unbroken relationship with God. When sin entered the human race, all of us were affected by the aftershock. From that moment forward, our will was bent on serving self. Our fallen nature is to become completely absorbed with self. In short, we live for self instead of God. Someone once said the smallest package in the world is a man wrapped up in himself. I tend to agree with that statement. If we are not careful, we hunters can be a selfish lot. This innate self-centered selfishness destroys our human relationships and the quality of life we all long to possess. We become driven to satisfy our own insatiable appetites for success, money, and pleasure. These appetites may be appeased short term, but our quests to satisfy them—goals realized, sexual pursuits, or money obtained never completely satisfy. No matter how successful one becomes, there is still that urge to see what's over the next hill. Thus, the unending pursuit of that ever illusive "something" continues.

There is only One who can truly fill the inner desires of the human spirit. There is only One who can calm the raging sea within. There is only One who brings the peace and contentment for which we long. There is only One who can heal shattered relationships. There is only One who can change us from the inside out. There is only One who gives life a new start. His name is Jesus.

When a person realizes they are broken and self-destructive—God is there. When a person realizes nothing satisfies the searching human heart—God is there. When a person acknowledges his own personal sin—God is there. What is God there to do?

God is there to reconcile (make right once again) your relationship with Him. This is what is commonly referred to as "salvation." While God does all the work during the salvation experience, there are essentially three criteria a person must exhibit in order to be "saved" (saved from the consequences of sin—a broken relationship with God now as well as in eternity—a place called Hell).

1. An individual must realize he is **separated from God** due to his personal sin.

2. An individual must be willing to **confess his sin** to God and **turn away** from it (repentance).

3. An individual must **surrender his "self"** to God and allow Jesus to be the head of his life from that point on.

Jesus paid the penalty of death for your sin when He died on the cross. Therefore, through his death/blood we can be reconciled (made right) with God.

When a person genuinely prays these things, God forgives his sin and supernaturally empowers him to turn away from sin.

However, we are not meant to live the Christian life alone. There is strength in numbers. The faith of others encourages us to remain strong. There is more to becoming a Christian than merely praying a prayer. Although you are now a Christian, you need to grow in this new faith. You need to learn how to lead others to follow Christ. This process of growth is called discipleship. Immediately, you need to tell someone of your new surrender to God. Ask the Lord to lead you to someone who can help you grow stronger in Him.

Please review the following verses for clarification:

1. Romans 10:1
2. John 3:16
3. Romans 3:23
4. Romans 5:8
5. Romans 10:9-11
6. Romans 10:13
7. John 4:23
8. 2 Timothy 2:2
9. Matthew 28:18-20

If you have accepted Christ through reading these devotionals or if they have helped your walk with the Lord, I am eager to hear from you. Please send your correspondence to:

Outdoor Reflections
c/o Tim E. Miller
2629 Cox Mill Rd.
Hopkinsville, KY 42240

e-mail dtn@bellsouth.net
Please indicate "Outdoor Reflections" as the subject.

New Contact Info:
Tim Miller
P.O. Box 157, Trenton, Ky 42286
Cell - 270-839-0649
dtn@hughes.net

About the Author

Tim Miller has hunted small and big game his entire life and successfully bagged grouse, quail, pheasants, ducks, geese, squirrels, rabbits, turkeys, whitetail deer, mule deer, elk and trapped a host of other furbearers. He also loves to fish, camp, and experience life in the great outdoors. Tim holds a Doctorate of Ministry degree and is president and founder of Disciple The Nations, Inc., a nonprofit international disciple making ministry. He lives with his wife, Lane Ann, and their four children in Hopkinsville, Kentucky.

For additional copies of this book, and information about Disciple The Nations, please visit www.disciplethenations.com.